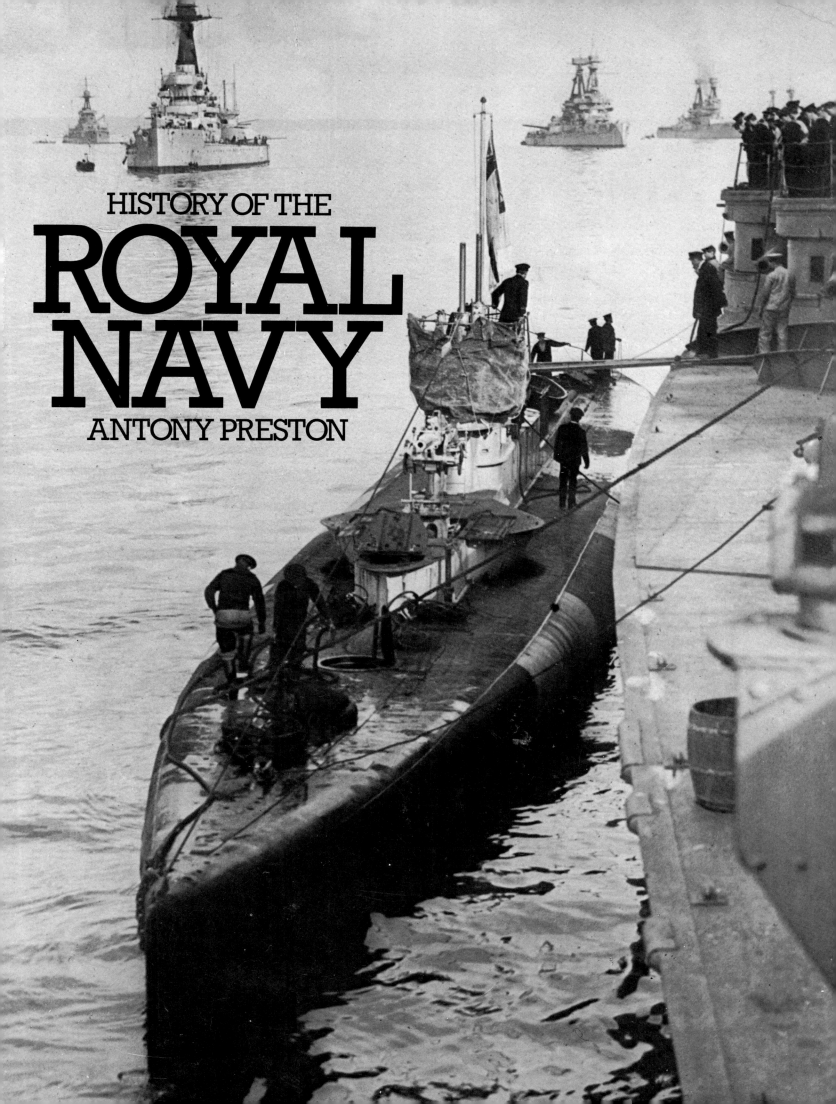

HISTORY OF THE
ROYAL
NAVY

ANTONY PRESTON

HISTORY OF THE
ROYAL NAVY

ANTONY PRESTON

HAMLYN
BISON

Published by
The Hamlyn Publishing Group Limited
London – New York – Sydney – Toronto
Astronaut House, Feltham
Middlesex, England

ISBN 0 600 38478 0

Produced by Bison Books Corp.
17 Sherwood Place,
Greenwich, CT 06830
USA.

Printed in Hong Kong

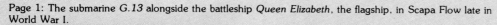

Page 1: The submarine *G.13* alongside the battleship *Queen Elizabeth*, the flagship, in Scapa Flow late in
World War I.
Page 2-3: The capture of St Lucia in the West Indies by a British squadron in February 1762.
This page: *MGB.511* at high speed while escorting a coastal convoy near the British Isles during World War II.

Contents

Introduction

It is difficult to know where to start on a one-volume history of the Royal Navy. With a string of campaigns, defeats and victories going back to the days of Alfred the Great, but taking in at the same time a breadth of experience which includes the two World Wars and their troubled aftermath, a comprehensive history would literally run to scores of volumes. So, with

some trepidation and awareness of my temerity in making the choice of what to put in and what to leave out, I have chosen to write about what I consider to be the most interesting aspects of the events which have befallen the British Navy since its astonishing defeat of the Armada of Spain nearly 400 years ago.

Purists may object that some very im-

portant events have been left out, but I would claim in self-defense that I have chosen actions which illustrate particular points in the narrative. For the reasons already outlined there must be deviations from a straight chronology, and if these sometimes seem arbitrary I can only ask for the reader's forbearance.

There are also those who might object to the inclusion of the Armada, on the grounds that the Navy which beat Spain was neither Royal nor British, but merely English. True, there was a Scottish Navy, which played no part in the fighting, but the forces gathered by Queen Elizabeth I were a national force, and their achievements mark the beginning of a tradition which survived unbroken to the 20th century.

The Battle of Trafalgar in 1805 set the seal on a British naval supremacy which lasted for more than a century.

In the following century the centralization of power made the formation of a truly British Navy possible, and it was left to Charles II to make it Royal. But above all it was geography which facilitated the growth of British sea power, for the British Isles lie in a commanding position off the north west coast of Europe, dominating the exits from the Baltic and the North Sea. Add to that the fortunate coincidence of prevailing winds blowing from the west and the majority of the good natural harbours being on the English side rather than the French side of the Channel and you have the foundations of British supremacy in the age of sail. The great French harbour of Brest was too far to the west to be able to offset the British advantage in safe anchorages, and the winds which kept British men o' war off the French coasts penned France's own in harbour. Even in the 20th century the pattern of weather favoured Britain; during the evacuation of Dunkirk and the D-Day landings, bad weather could be accurately forecast sooner in England than in Occupied France.

The origins of British seapower are usually claimed to be in the reign of King Alfred, when the Viking marauders from Scandinavia were checked for the first time. But even earlier, in the declining years of the Roman occupation, there had been a 'Count of the Saxon Shore' charged with the duty of defending the coast. We know very little about how Alfred's ships fought but we can be fairly sure that tactics were crude and the actions confined to local skirmishing. The ships and weapons had simply not evolved to the point where purely naval tactics could be imagined.

What is certain is that the lessons learned by Alfred the Great were not heeded by following generations of Saxons, for in 1066 William the Conqueror was able to bring his Norman knights and their destriers across the Channel without any hint of an attack by King Harold's ships, if they existed as a fighting force. Even as late as the 14th century the battles of l'Espagnols sur Mer and Sluys were not part of any developing naval strategy. They were simply extensions of the land warfare which was in progress, and had no decisive effect on the outcome of any campaign because of the relatively small numbers of men involved.

In later centuries it was said that Trade followed the Flag, but in a naval sense the Flag could only follow Trade, and it was not until English merchants began to trade beyond their own shores that any perception of sea power began to emerge. By Papal decree, Spain and Portugal had been given the New World to exploit, but where they had led others could follow, and when the science of navigation had advanced sufficiently, brave and unscrupulous English sailors began to venture abroad. This led inevitably to conflict and to protect this precious trade it was necessary to build ships which could defend themselves.

Since the days of Henry VIII and Queen Elizabeth I the fortunes of the British have therefore been inextricably linked with their Navy. Whenever the welfare of the Navy has been neglected, disaster has followed as surely as night follows day. And yet the Royal Navy has always shown remarkable powers of recovery, making the transition from peacetime neglect to wartime efficiency with rapidity, whereas the British Army has often taken several years to rid itself of peacetime thinking.

The Royal Navy has not only secured great gains for the nation by victories such as Trafalgar, but it has also saved temporary reverses from becoming total defeat. In recent times the evacuation of troops from Dunkirk and Crete were remarkable improvisations, but there were many more in previous centuries.

Surprisingly the British, as a great maritime nation which has reaped so much benefit from sea power, have taken a long time to appreciate the root causes of naval supremacy. As late as 1873 the Royal Naval College at Greenwich did not teach history as part of the curriculum. It was left to an American, Captain Mahan, to teach them the secret of their success, and another American, Professor Marder, produced the first penetrating analysis of the First World War at sea. Happily there is more appreciation of naval history in Great Britain today, which is as it should be.

The tide of empire has receded and today Great Britain is a much smaller and less important nation than it was even 40 years ago. Its navy reflects that decline in power and importance but the traditions die hard, and today the Royal Navy remains one of the most efficient in NATO. Even more important, its customs and attitudes were grafted onto healthy American stock, so that today the United States Navy shows the same understanding of sea power that was once a British monopoly.

The heavy cruiser *Suffolk* on patrol in the Denmark Strait in 1941. With HMS *Norfolk* she located the *Bismarck* and *Prinz Eugen,* averting a major onslaught on the Atlantic convoys.

The rise of British sea power can be traced back to the victory over the Spanish Armada.

The Armada

The long fight against Spain which culminated in the Armada actions in 1588 came at the right time for the fledgling English Navy. Although there had been no full action at sea since 1545 the English had benefited from the revolution in warship-design which had been in progress in northern Europe since about 1500. Henry VIII is often credited with developing the idea of 'piercing' the sides of his ships to take guns, although this is unlikely, as the design of a workable gunport with its hinged lid is credited to a Frenchman, Descharges. Be that as it may, the shipwright James Baker is credited with providing the answer to the King's instructions to find ways of getting the 'great guns' to sea, in the *Mary Rose* in 1513.

This single feature, combined with a break away from the medieval 'round ship' toward a longer hull form, less suited to cargo-carrying but more suited to fighting, marks not only a giant step forward for the English Navy but also a fundamental change in tactics. However crude these early guns might be their potential was as ship-killers rather than man-killers. Although ships like the *Mary Rose* still carried hundreds of longbows, the days of winning naval victories solely by boarding and entering were numbered.

It is appropriate that this turning point in British naval history should be well documented by the most important naval archeological discovery of recent times. In 1982, after a decade of painstaking work by a team of divers, nautical archeologists and salvage experts, the wreck of the *Mary Rose* was brought to the surface of the Solent near Portsmouth. She had been part of Henry VIII's great fleet putting to sea to engage the French in 1545 when, to the horror of the King and hundreds of spectators ashore, she heeled over and sank. Like the *Wasa* in Stockholm nearly 100 years later, she had heeled under a sudden gust of wind. Water had spilled over the sills of her gunports destroying her margin of stability.

Today it is possible to examine the work of Tudor shipwrights and marvel at the massive timbers of their ships, for the mud of the Solent has preserved about one-third of the original hull, including the sternpost. All manner of artefacts have also survived, including clothes, purses, compasses and even the contents of the surgeon's chest. Records of the Tudor Navy are fragmentary, and the recovery of the *Mary Rose* will help solve many of the mysteries about how ships were built and manned in the 16th century.

By 1588, when the long-standing religious and commercial rivalry between Protestant England and Catholic Spain had erupted into open war, the new technology of warship design had been mastered in northern Europe. Clearly Spain, as the world's leading maritime power, had both the money and the resources to match any development made by small countries like England and the Netherlands, but Spanish sea power had been so long wedded to the oared galley that the implications of the revolution were not heeded. Spanish tactics still relied on boarding and entering; like the Romans they sought to find a way in which they

could use their superior soldiery to overwhelm opposition at sea. However, they too put guns in their ships, and contrary to popular belief the Invincible Armada (its real name was 'la Felicissima Armada,' the most fortunate fleet) was better supplied with heavy 'demi-cannon' and 'periers' than the English Fleet. The real difference lay in the agility of the English ships, which had orders to attack *downwind* with gunfire; boarding without permission from the principal commander was expressly forbidden. The Spaniards took exactly the opposite view; they wanted to board, and their big galleons had land troops embarked for just that purpose. The only thing which prevented this from happening was the superior manoeuvrability of

Right: A model made from the only contemporary plans of an Elizabethan warship, possibly the *Elizabeth Jonas.*

Below left: The 'Most Fortunate Armada' leaving Ferrol on 12th July, 1588.

Below right: Contemporary view of the fight off the Isle of Wight.

the English men o' war, which simply failed to stay close enough to be boarded. Some measure of their success in avoiding serious damage can be guessed from the claimed figure of 100,000 round shot fired by the ships of the Armada, which accounted for only one ship, the pinnace *Delight*, her captain and some 20 seamen.

It is worth explaining at this point that the strength of the Felicissima Armada was well known to the English. The commander appointed by King Philip, the Duke of Medina Sidonia, had drawn up an elaborate list of the ships, their guns, the number of soldiers and even their personal weapons. Today it is inconceivable that such a detailed order of battle would not be highly classified, but the Spaniards were well aware of the propaganda value that their massive preparations would have. Even allowing for a measure of

Left: The great risk for English ships was to be drawn into close combat, where the Spanish weight of metal would tell.

Below left: Launch of the fireships, the move which broke the cohesion of the Armada.

Above: Lord Howard of Effingham, commander of Queen Elizabeth's fleet against the Armada.

exaggeration the force assembled was daunting. The First Line force comprised 10 Portuguese galleons, 10 Castilian galleons, 4 West Indiamen and 4 Neapolitan galleasses. The Second Line was made up of 40 large armed merchantmen and there were also 34 zabras, fregatas and pataches, most for scouting and carrying despatches, but a number reserved to screen the flagship *San Martin*. The Fleet Train included 23 urcas (supply ships) and 4 Portuguese galleys.

The Armada suffered terrible tribulations on its way north. While sheltering at Corunna the ships were lashed by a terrible storm, and the Duke had to wait until 21st July, nearly two months after leaving Lisbon, to collect all the stragglers. The dreaded 'ship fever' or typhus had already begun to infect the ranks of soldiery, and an increasing amount of spoiled food and water was being discovered. The English, fretting at the Queen's niggardliness, were convinced that they faced 500 ships and 80,000 men in magnificent fighting condition. Had they but known, Medina Sidonia's problems were simply their own, but magnified.

The first contact was made on 29th July, by the bark *Golden Hind* off the Scilly Isles. By the time Drake and Howard could get their ships out of Plymouth late that evening the Spanish were already beating up the Channel. In theory they had caught the English at a tactical disadvantage, holding the weather-gauge and the enemy trapped in harbour by wind and tide, but they did not reckon on the superb seamanship of Lord Howard's West Country sailors, who knew these Channel waters so well.

The Spaniards adopted an unusual crescent formation, which meant that enemy ships trying to keep the weather-gauge ran the risk of being trapped by the horns. This restricted them to attacking the extremities, and here the Duke had placed his most powerful ships. The only alternative was to bring on a general melée, in which case the Spanish had every hope of success. Against this the

Above: The *White Bear*.

English could only hope to play picador to the Spanish bull, using their culverins to batter the enemy at long range where they were safe from boarding.

The first engagement seems to have started by accident, when the Vice Admiral Juan Martinez de Recalde in the galleon *San Juan de Portugal* turned to meet the attack of Drake in the *Revenge*, Hawkins in the *Victory* and Frobisher in the *Triumph*. Perhaps the wily Recalde hoped that he could grapple and board one of the English galleons, tempting the rest of the fleet to come to her rescue, and precipitating the sort of melée which the

Below: Bearer of one of the most famous names in the Royal Navy's history, the flagship *Ark Royal*.

Spanish wanted. But the English held off at 300 yards or more (some indication of how short-ranged the guns of the 16th century really were), and bombarded the *San Juan* for more than an hour. After a sore battering she was finally rescued by the *Grangrin* and other ships of her squadron.

The English had failed, however, in their aim of inflicting serious damage on the Armada, whose seamanship and discipline remained impeccable. The English heavy guns, principally 18-pounder 'whole culverins' and 9-pounder 'demi-culverins' were too light to penetrate the Spanish ships' massive timbers. Analysis of the running fight up the Channel reveals that only three ships were seriously damaged, of which two were captured. One of these, the *Nuestra Señora del Rosario* was captured after

being disabled in a collision, while the *San Salvador* was badly damaged by an explosion of gunpowder.

The story of Francis Drake playing a last game of bowls on Plymouth Hoe may be apocryphal but it underlines the dogged rearguard action fought by Lord Howard of Effingham and his lieutenant. Not until the Armada was committed to the Channel did Howard order his ships to attack, and as we have seen, Drake, Hawkins and Frobisher were prepared to fight cautiously. However, it could never be forgotten that the Duke of Medina Sidonia's strategic objective was to reach Flanders, where his ships could embark the Duke of Parma's mighty army and then carry it across to England. Viewed in that light the Armada had come a long way toward achieving its aims when it reached Calais on the night of 6th August. But the cost had been heavy, for although the Spanish ships were still in formation and had not suffered further losses, they had fired away most of their round shot.

The following night the English sent in hastily prepared fireships, eight small ships packed with combustible materials such as pitch. With their guns doubleshotted, ready to fire when the heat reached them, to increase the amount of damage and confusion, and rudders lashed, the fireships were sent on their way, set aflame and abandoned to follow wind and tide into Calais. As always the threat of fire was sufficient for every Spanish ship to cut her cable and make for the open sea. The disciplined formation of the Armada had finally been broken, and the English were quick to seize the advantage. In the ensuing Battle of Gravelines there was at last a close-fought action, but by now the English ships were very low on powder and shot, and after four hours of bloody fighting they broke off the action without achieving decisive victory. Nonetheless the galleass *San Lorenzo* and another ship had been driven ashore. Only a friendly wind which blew the English ships out of range saved others from suffering a similar fate. In fact the wind saved the Armada, for during the night of 8-9 August it blew harder and harder, blowing the Spanish ships before it and leaving the English far behind. Finally the Duke bowed to the inevitable, and despairing of any joint operation with Parma, decided to try to extricate his fleet without completing King Philip's Great Enterprise.

The result was tragedy. With no further intervention from the English the Armada battled its way around the the north west of Scotland, still one of the worst sea passages in northern Europe. With scurvy and typhus taking a constant toll of seamen and soldiers, it became a struggle to

Far right: The Dutch artist Visscher's engraving of the *Ark Royal*.

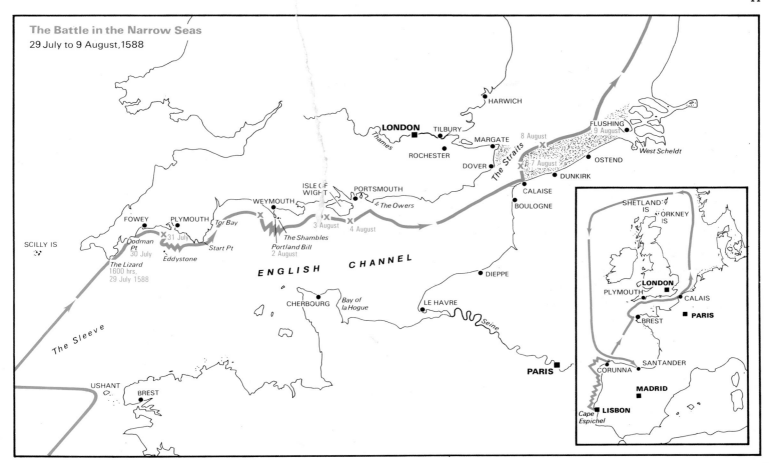

The Battle in the Narrow Seas
29 July to 9 August, 1588

get any ships home. Up until 13th August seven first line ships had been lost and the remainder were so badly damaged that they could not be regarded as fit to face a long voyage. A fifth of the men were dead or wounded and they were virtually out of ammunition. Worse, there was no more fresh food, and the biscuit and salted meat and fish were rotten. Water was desperately short, the worst problem of all.

Incredibly the Duke and his captains managed to save something from the disaster, for by rights none should have got home. Roughly half of the ships, 66 out of the 130 which had left the Tagus, reached home ports by the end of September. Storm and wreck had achieved what Elizabeth's Navy had failed to do.

The worst losses had been off the wild west coast of Ireland. Five out of seven ships which tried to find shelter there survived. At least seventeen more perished on the way to Ireland, but contrary to popular belief the natives of Galway treated the survivors well. According to the leading authority there is only one example of the native Irish killing castaways; other atrocities were committed at the behest of English landlords.

The consequences of the Armada's destruction for England were far-reaching. The country was now free from the threat of invasion, and her maritime trade would also benefit from the rebuff to Spain. But above all the 'tradition of victory' had been established. Elizabeth I was hardly a visionary where sea power was concerned, for she spent as little

money as possible on the Queen's Ships. Her successor James I was even more niggardly, but in the minds of the English (and later the Scots and Welsh as well) the defeat of the Armada was seen as a triumph of the weak over the strong.

It was fertile soil for mythology, and even today the popular view is that small English ships defeated much bigger Spanish ships by devastating gunpower. 'God blew with His winds and they were scattered' made a resounding legend for a commemorative gold medallion, and it might be unkind to point out that the wind which allowed the Spaniards to escape

Overleaf: Engravings of two phases of the action off the Isle of Wight. The crescent formation of the Armada is well shown in the left-hand map.

from Gravelines must have been at least welcomed by the Duke of Medina Sidonia. But these are the quibbles of modern revisionist historians, and the defeat of the Armada must be remembered as the first large-scale English *national* victory at sea. There was not yet a British nation nor yet a Royal Navy, but 1588 marks the foundation stone for both institutions.

War Against the Dutch

The Four Days' Fight, 1-4 June 1666, a bloody encounter between the new Royal Navy and the Dutch.

Despite their reprieve from the vengeance of Spain the haughty islanders had scarcely begun to enjoy the fruits of their great victory before their leaders began to neglect the instrument of that victory. King James VI and I was a do-gooder, a unilateral disarmer so aware of the horrors of war that he decided to set a good example by disarming his own country first. There may have been sound fiscal and economic reasons for bringing the 19-year-old Spanish War to a close but he also crippled the nation's ability to wage maritime war in the future. Privateering was already a well-established practice whereby a private citizen or group of citizens was permitted to furnish and arm a ship to prey upon the enemy's commerce. To distinguish such private enterprise efforts from mere piracy on the high seas, the privateer captain had to be

issued with a 'Letter of Marque' from the Crown. When King James refused to issue any more Letters of Marque he was undoubtedly striking a blow for the freedom of the seas and for more civilized behaviour, but as so often happens the enemy merely saw it as a suicidal gesture. As no other nation followed the English lead this left the growing English mercantile fleet vulnerable to privateering, while her enemies were free of any such threat.

As this quixotic gesture was accompanied by neglect of the fine navy bequeathed by Queen Elizabeth, the results were disastrous. English (and Scottish, now that the two kingdoms were ruled by the same monarch) shipping was plundered by every type of marauder, even in the English Channel, and commercial rivals like the Dutch ousted English traders from those areas which the Elizabethans had wrested from Spain.

The problem was a deep-rooted one, partly financial and partly administrative. The English Crown was permanently short of money, and although makeshift

policies had sufficed through to the end of the 16th century, the growing expense of central government demanded some better way of funding defence. Good Queen Bess had used the profit from her merchant adventurers' exploits to pay for her fighting ships but King James could not bring himself to use such methods. As another government was to try to do in 1981, his solution was to cut the Navy to the bone.

Charles I, who followed James I, has been damned for all time as a Good Man but a Bad King, but he was not so bad that he could not see the dangers of neglecting the Navy. His notorious attempt to levy the 'ship-money' tax was to spark off the Civil War, but we ought to remember that the principle in dispute between King and Parliament was not whether or not to have a State-funded Navy, but the more fundamental question of whether that Navy ought to belong to the Nation or the King. It was Charles' mistake to get these two issues hopelessly entangled, for he subscribed to already obsolete notions of the

Below: In the Four Days' Fight, the English lost more ships and men than the Dutch but their superior discipline saved them.

divine right of kingship at a time when his unruly subjects had equally strong notions about the need to preserve their civil liberties. The outcome of the Civil War was, as we know, the defeat of the Royalists, the execution of King Charles and the triumph of Parliament – albeit at the will of the New Model Army. Before the constitutional crisis flared into open hostilities, however, King Charles had secured an important concession from Parliament. The first ship-money levied was actually spent on new warships, and the English could now boast a small but comparatively efficient national navy, the immediate forebear of the Royal Navy.

The rollcall of the English Civil War goes on at great length about the battles on land, but in a sense the outcome was decided by the Navy. By refusing to side with the King the sailors made it impossible for the French or any other European power to bring aid to the Royalists. Later, in the second phase of the Civil War, the Navy's loyalty did split but the two halves virtually cancelled one another out as

factors in the struggle and the effect was the same – the outcome of the war was decided without foreign intervention.

Once hostilities were over Parliament took immediate steps to get control over the Navy, for it recognised how much it owed to the sailors' allegiance, or at least how easily the sailors might have tipped the balance against them. Using a far more ruthless scale of taxation than Charles I would have dared to exact, a new and formidable fleet was built. Thus when the military reality behind Parliament, the New Model Army and its commander Oliver Cromwell, took over control, an ideal instrument of foreign policy had been forged. The Commonwealth government, with its puritanical laws and military rule, was hardly popular with the masses, and like most dictators Cromwell was glad to divert popular dislike from himself to a third party. This was Holland, once the oppressed Protestant ally in the struggle against Spain but now an ambitious and dangerous commercial rival. Means, motive and opportunity were to hand, and so war with the Dutch became inevitable. The First Dutch War, which began in 1653, was noteworthy for the first use of a

Above: George Monck, later Duke of Albemarle, was the ablest of Cromwell's 'Generals at Sea' and served his restored King equally well.

formal line of battle. The reason for this innovation was the shortage of experienced sea-officers (most were Royalists); Cromwell had been forced to appoint a series of 'Generals at Sea', Blake, Deane and Popham, as Commissioners of the Navy. These makeshift admirals deplored the melée, which was the accepted form of battle, and instituted a more disciplined formation in order to make better use of gunpower to offset Dutch ship-handling skills. It is amusing to think of these soldiers-turned-sailors plotting parade ground manoeuvres but in fact these were logical and necessary improvements. They took advantage of the bigger and better-armed ships now being built, and the reforms had the blessing of Vice Admiral Sir William Penn, the Navy's most experienced commander.

Blake and his fellow Commissioners also turned their attention to the equally vital matter of logistics and support, clearing the dockyards of as much corruption

Left: Phineas Pett and his masterpiece, the 100-gun 1st Rate *Sovereign of the Seas*. She was launched in 1637.

Right: The daring raid known as 'Holmes' Bonfire' in 1666 burned large numbers of Dutch ships.

and inefficiency as possible. Arrears of pay were paid and the rations were improved, and as a result men were found to man three squadrons. These ships gave a good account of themselves in chasing the Royalist squadron under Prince Rupert out of English waters.

Today Robert Blake is still remembered as one of England's naval heroes, for he did much to restore the reputation of the English Navy to the pinnacle which it had reached in 1588. He achieved his successes at a time when the Dutch were commanded by one of their most brilliant sailors, Marten Tromp, and yet had to endure the bitterness of defeat.

Both sides were spoiling for a fight by May 1652. The pretext was the appearance of Tromp's squadron in the Downs, the sheltered anchorage for English shipping in the Channel; Blake arrived the following day, demanded a salute, and when it was not forthcoming fired a warning shot. This was answered by a broadside from the *Brederode* against Blake's flagship the *James* (50 guns). After five hours of heavy fighting the Dutch withdrew, having caused heavy damage to Blake's flagship. Although an indecisive battle it was a worthy achievement by Blake, who had first gone to sea at the age of fifty, to hold his own against the most outstanding fighter afloat.

Blake did better when he met De Witt and De Ruyter off the North Foreland the following September, but the Dutch did not give in easily, and the Estates General voted funds to fit out a large fleet. Although it may be hard to credit, the Commonwealth parliament, instead of doing likewise, reduced the fleet and returned the merchant ships to their owners. As a result Blake had to face Tromp's one hundred ships with only forty off Dungeness at the end of November 1652. As was to be expected the Dutch won, and it was after this engagement that Tromp is said to have hoisted a broom to the masthead, claiming that he had swept the English from the seas.

The Commissioners of the Navy had been concerned about the apparent lack of tactical discipline shown at Dungeness, and set about making some changes. The Council of State confirmed Blake in command, but appointed another successful

Left: The 70-gun 3rd Rate HMS *Resolution* of 1667, in a gale.

Right: The reply to 'Holmes' Bonfire' was de Ruyter's attack on the Medway the following year, which concluded the Second Dutch War.

26

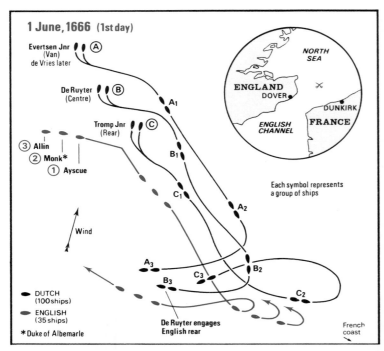

1 June, 1666 (1st day)

Evertsen Jnr (Van) de Vries later — Ⓐ

De Ruyter (Centre) — Ⓑ

Tromp Jnr (Rear) — Ⓒ

③ Allin
② Monk *
① Ayscue

A₁ B₁ C₁ A₂ A₃ B₃ C₃ B₂ C₂

Wind

NORTH SEA
ENGLAND DOVER
ENGLISH CHANNEL
DUNKIRK
FRANCE

Each symbol represents a group of ships

⬤ DUTCH (100 ships)
⬤ ENGLISH (35 ships)

* Duke of Albemarle

De Ruyter engages English rear

French coast

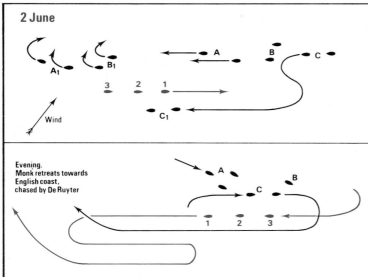

2 June

A B C
A₁ B₁
3 2 1
C₁

Wind

Evening. Monk retreats towards English coast, chased by De Ruyter

A B C
1 2 3

3 June: Monk continues retreat westward followed by De Ruyter. 'Royal Prince' runs aground on Galloper Shoal and is taken by Tromp. Rupert's squadron rejoins English fleet.

4 June

Van Ness with Tromp following gives chase to 3 or 4 English ships

C₁ 1 2 3 4
2₁ 3₁ 4₁
A₁ B₁ A B C
1₁ Two fleets exchange broadsides for two hours

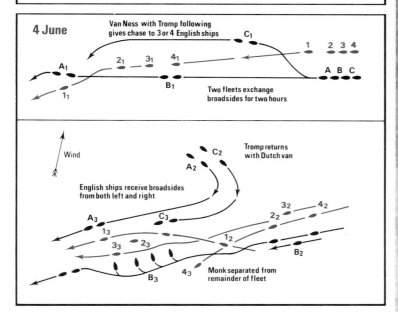

Wind

C₂ A₂ Tromp returns with Dutch van

English ships receive broadsides from both left and right

A₃ C₃ 3₂ 4₂
1₃ 2₂
3₃ 2₃ 1₂
4₃ B₂
B₃ Monk separated from remainder of fleet

soldier, George Monck, to be a 'General at Sea.' To remedy the shortage of men 1200 soldiers were drafted into the Navy, the first of what was to become the elite corps of marines. New Fighting Instructions were drafted and promulgated by March 1653, in time for the next Dutch clash.

On 2nd June 1653 Monck used a line ahead formation to inflict a severe defeat on Tromp at the Gabbard Bank. The Dutch still pinned their hopes on boarding and entering, and their report on the battle specifically mentions the power of the English guns and Blake's refusal to resort to boarding tactics.

Another reform tested by the Gabbard battle was the new code of discipline created to deal with insubordination of the type shown at the Battle of Dungeness. The conduct of some of Blake's captains in that battle had been nothing less than disgraceful. A portion of his fleet had been composed of commandeered merchant ships, and when they saw the heavy odds ranged against them they left the scene as fast as they could. But in spite of deserting their commander in the face of danger, the

Left: The attack by Sir Robert Holmes on Dutch shipping lying in the Vlie, on 20 August, 1666. 150 merchantmen were destroyed.

Below: Captain Kempthorn's frigate *Mary Rose* in action against seven Algerine pirate ships in 1669.

legal theory of 'Droits of Admiralty' did not permit their commander to take action against them, only to report them to the Government. Under the monarchy the Lord High Admiral had in theory led the Fleet to sea in person, and so exercised authority directly, but this had, of course, been a legal fiction for many years.

The answer was a totally new code of conduct or 'Articles of War' governing the conduct of the Navy at sea. This momentous piece of legislation was drafted and enacted within a month of the Battle of Dungeness and it put responsibility fairly and squarely where it belonged, on the shoulders of the Commander of the Fleet. Incidentally in recognition of the legal nicety whereby one of the 'Droits of Admiralty' was now ceded to the Commander, the cumbersome term 'General-at-Sea' was immediately replaced by 'Admiral.'

The Battle of Scheveningen on 31st July 1653, sometimes known as the First Battle of the Texel, marked not only a convincing victory for the English Fleet but also the end of the First Dutch War. Marten Tromp was killed, and like all Anglo-Dutch sea battles it was a bloody affair.

The Second Dutch War of 1665-1667 was fought under the restored monarchy but with the ships and men of Cromwell's Navy. The King's brother, the Duke of York, commanded the Fleet in the first engagement, the Battle of Lowestoft in

June 1665, but the ablest commander was undoubtedly George Monck, now ennobled as the Duke of Albemarle for assisting in the Restoration. Unfortunately in this war the English tacticians were split into two factions: 'Formalists' who adhered to the Instructions of 1653 and 'Meléeists', who trusted to English gunnery and seamanship to give victory ship-for-ship. The Battle of Lowestoft was a formal engagement which was insufficiently decisive, according to the Duke of York's critics.

The meléeists had their chance in the 'Four Days' Fight', so called because it lasted from 1-4 June 1666. Albemarle put his ideas into practice competently enough, but ship-for-ship superiority did not help as the Dutch Admiral de Ruyter outnumbered him nearly two-to-one. It was a terrible slogging match, with neither side willing to cry off. Although the Dutch did eventually withdraw it could not by any criterion be called an English victory,

The three-decker *Royal Prince* was built in 1670. In 1694, the ship was rebuilt and renamed *Royal William*.

with ten of Albemarle's ships sunk against De Ruyter's six, and nearly 4000 casualties.

Many of the Duke of Albemarle's contemporaries called him a hothead, but the old soldier had shown a remarkable degree of tactical skill. Even more amazing was his fleet's power of recovery, for only seven weeks later the English Fleet fell upon the Dutch near the North Foreland and defeated them decisively. The St James's Day Fight, as it was known, did nothing to settle the debate between the advocates of line tactics and the melee, but it did restore English fortunes. In spite of all the hard knocks the war did seem to be about to end in another crushing defeat for the Dutch. To set the seal on the victory Sir Robert Holmes was despatched with

'Honest Benbow' was Master of the Fleet at Beachy Head in 1690 and at La Hogue in 1692. He died of wounds in the West Indies in 1702.

nine frigates and a squadron of fireships to attack shipping lying in the Vlie. The raid succeeded in destroying some 150 ships, and English pamphleteers gloatingly referred to 'Holmes' Bonfire.'

As at the end of the previous war financial considerations now took over, not just from military needs but from ordinary common sense and logic. To save money the King gave orders that the Fleet was to be laid up 'In Ordinary' (reserve), at Chatham, on the assumption that the Dutch were too exhausted to make any further effort, and because peace was believed to be imminent. The only form of insurance against disaster was to begin a laborious process of fortifying the Medway and Portsmouth. This may have made sense to the King and his financial advisers, but to the Dutch, burning to avenge 'Holmes' Bonfire', it appeared to be a heaven-sent chance to reverse the course of the war. On the night of 7th June 1667 a fleet of sixty ships under De Ruyter anchored off the mouth of the Thames. Light forces were then sent up the Medway to attack Sheerness and to sink any shipping lying in the river. Five days of panic-stricken countermeasures were useless, and not even the arrival of the Duke of Albemarle was sufficient to stiffen the defences. On the night of 12th June De Ruyter's ships arrived, brushing aside the defences with disdain. Chatham Dockyard suffered heavily, with several ships set on fire and some of the finest ships in the Navy, the *Royal James* (82), *Loyal London* (90) and the *Royal Oak* (76) being destroyed at their moorings. Most humiliating of all, the 90-gun *Royal Charles* was towed back to Holland.

Needless to say, the peace treaty

agreed at Breda the following month was considerably more favourable to the Dutch than it might have been. Some measure of the effect on English morale can be gauged from the choice of this incident as a comparable humiliation by the leader-writer of *The Times* when in 1942 the newspaper attacked the Admiralty and the Churchill government for allowing the *Scharnhorst* and *Gneisenau* to pass through the English Channel in broad daylight. Amid all the setbacks suffered, the burning of the Fleet at Chatham remains a most disgraceful episode in the minds of the British and the Royal Navy.

Before we close the subject of the First and Second Dutch Wars it is important to look at the administrative machine which was evolving. The return of Charles II to his throne in 1660 did not result in all the reforms of the Commonwealth being swept away, but it did usher in further radical changes. Charles re-created for a time the office of Lord High Admiral and bestowed it on his younger brother, the Duke of York. James threw himself into the task with great zeal, and in his work he had the benefit of an outstanding assistant, the Clerk of the Acts to the Navy Board, Samuel Pepys.

Pepys was a most remarkable man, for although he had no practical experience of the dockyards, nor even any sea-experience, he was a born administrator. Given a free hand by the Duke, he methodically set about reforming the administrative machinery of the Navy Board. The work that he did was to transform not only the administrative methods but the Navy itself, and during his long term of office the Navy at last became 'Royal' in name.

King Charles, for all his faults, took a keen interest in the Navy and frequently intervened in matters of policy. In 1668 he appointed a Committee of the Navy with himself presiding, and this in effect put an end to the Lord High Admiral's function as Commander of the Fleet. When his brother was forced to resign in 1673 the King revived the office of Lord High Admiral, but in his own person as head of a new Board of Admiralty, with the indispensable Mr Pepys as Secretary to the Board.

Strange as it may seem, there had never before been a formal structure of this kind, to formulate and execute naval policy, to appoint officers, and above all, to keep records. All this was achieved by Pepys, and in effect he shaped single-handed the Royal Navy's administration for the next 150 years or more. The old Navy Board was retained, but more and more it was given the technical tasks: running the dockyards, preparing designs for new ships and manning and victualling the Fleet. Significantly, the secret of Pepys' success was that for much of the time he was running both the Admiralty Board and the Navy Board, so that the two departments ran in the closest harmony.

The new administrative system was severely tested in the Third Dutch War, which had actually started the year before the King started his programme of reforms. It was also the Royal Navy's misfortune still to be suffering from the savage humiliation of the attack on the

Below: Dunkirk, the French port in contention throughout the wars between Britain and France. This engraving shows a raid in April 1713.

Above and below: The Battle of La Hogue in 1692, also known as Barfleur, was a resounding victory for the English and Dutch over the French.

Medway, as the hunt for scapegoats which followed resulted in pressure on the administrators rather than their Royal master, who had caused the catastrophe.

The war itself started, inevitably, as a reprisal for a provocative action. Once again Sir Robert Holmes was involved, this time in demanding a salute from a Dutch squadron escorting a convoy home from the Mediterranean. The salute was refused, a gun was fired, and a three-day running fight ensued. Once again it was a hard-fought war, with bloody actions and long casualty lists. Solebay on 28th May 1672 and the Second Battle of the Texel on 11th August 1673 were both fought to the finish and in each case de Ruyter's seamanship and tactical sense enabled him to escape defeat. However, the outcome of this long series of wars was a strategic defeat of the Dutch. They failed to dominate the English Channel and the southern half of the North Sea, their main aim throughout. Being a small country on the mainland of Europe, Holland's land frontier had to be given as much attention as her sea defences, whereas the English had all the benefits of being an island, as well as a gift of geography – being perfectly placed to block both the northern and southern exits from the North Sea. That combination was to prove even more useful during the next 250 years.

Pour Encourager
Les Autres

In 1745, the first attempt to take the French fortress of Louisburg on Cape Breton Island was a failure. The fortress remained in French hands for another 13 years.

Given the well-oiled administrative machinery bequeathed by Samuel Pepys, it might be expected that the Admiralty and the Royal Navy would go from strength to strength. Reality, however, was very different, and the advance of the 18th century saw a new breed of political admirals who owed their allegiance first to one or other political party, Whigs or Tories. This meant at best that for many years Whig officers stood a better chance of promotion than Tories, for as long as the Whig Ascendancy lasted, and merit came a poor second. Even more vicious, however, was the elevation of the Permanent Fighting Instructions to a level where they became mandatory (and, as the name says, permanent) rather than merely advisory. Maintaining the formal line of battle became the sole aim of a naval action, and it called for an exceptionally daring captain to break out of his admiral's formed line. The result was a series of indecisive actions in which opportunities to achieve a tactical surprise were deliberately thrown away to avoid breaking the line. It has been pointed out by no less an authority than Professor Michael Lewis that no British fleet inflicted a decisive defeat upon an enemy squadron between the Battle of Barfleur in 1692 and the Battle of the Saintes at the end of the American War in 1782.

Such a degree of timidity seems hard to credit in a service which had spent the previous 50 years fighting the Dutch, and looked to its defeat of the Armada another 50 years back, but the facts speak for themselves. The reason was obvious: the fate of those who ignored the Permanent Instructions without producing some sort of victory was swift and unpleasant. Admiral Mathews, the Commander in Chief of the Mediterranean Fleet, was court-martialled after an action off Toulon in February 1744, along with his second in command Vice-Admiral Richard Lestock and eleven captains. Seven captains were dismissed or suspended but in spite of overwhelming evidence to prove that Lestock had deliberately refused to support his superior in battle, he was acquitted while Mathews was cashiered. Even if we ignore inferences that Lestock had been acquitted because of his political connections, the real injustice was that Mathews' main crime was seen by the Navy to be his breach of the Permanent Instructions.

Even worse was the fate meted out to Admiral John Byng. When he fought an action with the French off Minorca in May 1756, at a crucial point in the battle he refused to break his own line, and missed a chance to relieve the beleaguered British garrison ashore. Instead he tamely returned to Gibraltar, leaving the redcoats to surrender the vital fortress and naval dockyard, the Royal Navy's only base inside the Mediterranean.

The Admiralty had no power to court martial Byng for cowardice or negligence in returning to Gibraltar, as he was technically not 'in the face of the enemy.' But they could indict him for his conduct of the battle, and inevitably he was found guilty of negligence (he was, however, acquitted of cowardice). Sadly the death-penalty had been made mandatory for the lesser offence in 1749, and as the King

Right: The notorious action off Toulon in February 1744, which resulted in courts martial for two admirals and 11 captains.

Far right: The Battle of Cape Passaro in 1718, between Sir George Byng and a Spanish squadron.

Below left: Plan of the Toulon action, showing the English and French line of battle.

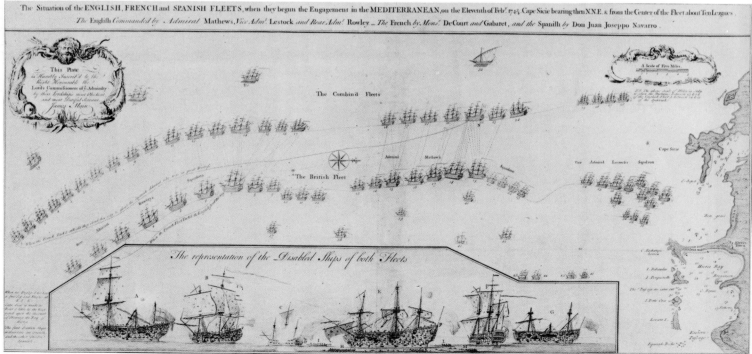

36

Above: Rowlandson's view of Portsmouth in 1790 shows the turmoil of the Royal Navy's premier dockyard.

Above: A portrait of Lord Graham in his cabin by Hogarth *c.*1740.

chose for political reasons not to exercise the prerogative of mercy, poor Byng had to die. He was executed on the quarter-deck of a battleship by a firing squad, a miscarriage of justice which prompted Voltaire's *bon mot* about shooting an admiral from time to time *pour encourager les autres.*

The miracle was that the Royal Navy still managed to breed officers who could rise above the system. Some experimenters tried to adhere as closely as possible to the concept of the unbreakable line, but using a series of Additional Instructions to give commanders greater freedom. Vernon, Anson, Boscawen, Hawke and Rodney were innovators in this category, and although they never managed completly to break the tyranny of the line, they did win back some of the independence which had been stripped from commanders.

The change was gradual, but the degree to which matters had improved was demonstrated by the outcome of what came to be called the 'Keppel-Palliser Affair.' The Honourable Augustus Keppel, an Admiral of the Blue, had fought an indecisive action with the French off Ushant during the War of American Independence in July 1778. As in the Mathews-Lestock Affair 34 years earlier, Keppel found that his subordinate, Vice-Admiral Sir Hugh Palliser, was clearly reluctant to obey his request for support. One might think that Palliser would have been court-martialled but the bold Sir Hugh was able to persuade the Board to court-martial Keppel. The charges were carefully worded to ensnare Keppel but fortunately the court martial threw them all out, and Palliser was brought to book instead, and found guilty of both insubordination and negligence.

What the 18th century naval tactician lacked was an adequate code of signals. Originally a fixed set of signals had been

Near and far right: The front and back of the Harrison chronometer, an accurate timepiece used in navigation.

Near and far right: The front and back of the Harrison chronometer, an accurate timepiece used in navigation.

incorporated in the Permanent Fighting Instructions but as these Instructions had grown in complexity the problem of coping with the appropriate signals had grown too. For example, a captain seeing a flag hoist flying from the flagship's yard-arm had to locate and identify the flags from the relevant page of the Instructions. Admiral Howe tackled the problem and issued a Signal Book for his own squadron in 1776 – merely placing the signals in alphabetical order made it much easier to identify them. But there was no official backing for such unorthodoxy, and for some years the only copies afloat were privately compiled.

There was one more pernicious result of the Admiralty's hardened arteries of decision-making. The design of warships, particularly those 'great ships', the towering two- and three-deckers, had been largely a matter of guesswork until the 17th century. We know that attempts were being made to record data in the form of building plans; technical drawings of an unnamed Elizabethan galleon (tentatively identified as the *Elizabeth Jonas*) were included in Matthew Baker's *Fragments of Ancient Shipwrightry* before the Armada battle. In 1684 Thomas Keltridge drew up plans for several representative ship-types, and clearly Pepys began a process of keeping technical records. 'Establishments', the legally fixed strength of the Navy in any given year, began to be drawn up toward the end of the 17th century, with the number of the various classes, 1st Rates, 2nd Rates, 3rd Rates etc, voted by Parliament. From that point it was a logical step to define each 'rate' by length, beam and tonnage to ensure that Parliament got the type of ship for which it had paid. Certainly in Pepys' time, if not before, the practice of building a Navy Board model of each prototype was introduced, and there is a painting in the National Maritime Museum of King Charles II and his ministers examining a model of a new 1st Rate before approving its building.

Parliament was always niggardly with money, and so the 'Establishment' dimensions for the early 18th century were kept as small as possible. As a result captains began to complain that their ships were inferior to the enemy's, particularly the French. The Navy Board was aware of these criticisms and as the years went by the Establishment dimensions were re-

Right: Admiral John Byng was the son of Sir George Byng, created Lord Torrington after the Battle of Cape Passaro.

Left: The execution of Byng on the quarterdeck of HMS *Monarch* in March 1757.

vised upward, but it is interesting to note that the main failing of English men o' war of the early 18th century was that they carried too many guns for their size, not that they were under-armed.

Things did get better and by the middle of the 18th century the restrictions of the Establishment dimensions were discarded. An enduring myth exists that all 18th century British warships were slow and under-armed by comparison with their French counterparts; then and now, critics cite the number of captured French ships taken into service with the Royal Navy as proof of the superiority of French designs. Modern research has thrown a lot of interesting light on this viewpoint, and mid-century Navy Board records present a very different picture. The reports on ex-French prizes show a rising tide of criticism, claiming that they are too lightly built for British service, insufficiently stored for long cruises, and above all, too lightly armed. What emerges is a sharp difference in emphasis; in the Royal Navy ship-design emphasised robustness for operations in a broad range of weather conditions and at a great distance from home, whereas the French, who had less and less hope of challenging the British in numbers, concentrated on building a fleet for intervention and the harassment of trade. Over the years this resulted in ships built to sally out on specific missions of interdiction, capable of sailing fast under specific conditions, but not suited for sustained operations in all weathers. What the French do deserve much credit for is their pioneer work in developing the science of naval architecture, whereas the

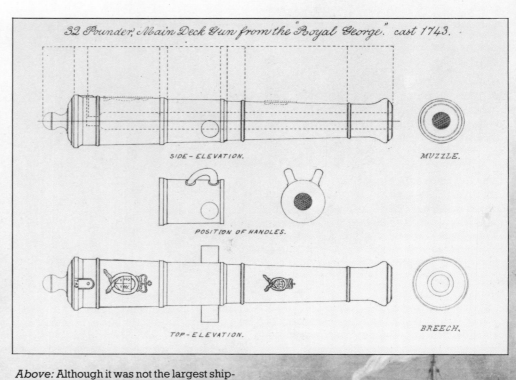

32 Pounder, Main Deck Gun from the "Royal George", cast 1743.

SIDE-ELEVATION.

MUZZLE.

POSITION OF HANDLES.

TOP-ELEVATION.

BREECH.

Above: Although it was not the largest ship-gun in the Royal Navy, the 32-pounder (6.3-inch calibre) proved most effective and saw wide service.

A SHIP *of War, of the third Rate, With Rigging &c. at Anchor.*

Section *of a SHIP of War, of y.º First Rate, Shewing y.º Inside.*

Above: Rigging plan of a 3rd Rate, *c.* 1700. What may appear to be a tangle of ropes was, in fact, a complex wind-machine.

Below: The burning of Payta in November 1741, one of a number of raids on enemy possessions.

Left: A cartoonist's view of the Press Gang, *c.*1790. The Press mainly operated when trained seamen could not be found.

Below: The bombardment of Bastia in 1745.

an officer's (and ordinary sailor's) perquisite going back to the days of Queen Elizabeth I and earlier, and if a captain could persuade the Admiralty to buy his prize and take her into the Royal Navy his reward (and each officer's and sailor's share) was even bigger, for he was deemed to have saved the Admiralty the cost of buying a new warship. There was also the understandable tendency to enhance one's achievement by exaggerating the fighting power of the opponent. What was often ignored was a disparity of gunpower, for a British 38-gun ship was not necessarily inferior to a French 40-gun ship. The weight of shot was used to measure the calibre of a gun, and a

British were content to rely on a rule-of-thumb approach. The French experimented constantly with unusual hull-forms, whereas the British tended to make piecemeal improvements to well-proven designs.

According to one modern authority, Robert Gardiner, the peak of British warship design was probably in the 1750s and 1760s, when Sir Thomas Slade was Surveyor of the Navy. Nor can it be dismissed as a coincidence that Slade's series of brilliant designs fought with distinction in the Seven Years' War. The ship for which he is remembered is the 100-gun 1st Rate HMS *Victory*, for although she is best known as Nelson's flagship at Trafalgar her real fame ought to be that she was an exceptionally fast 1st Rate without equal. Copies of the *Victory* were being added to the class ten years after Slade's death in 1771.

Slade's successors, Sir John Williams and Sir Edward Hunt, did not have the same flair and were by and large content to build ships along the same lines, but lacking the superb sailing qualities of the originals. The differences between French and British philosophy can be seen most clearly in the frigates of the 1770s and 1780s, fast single-decked ships intended to operate on their own, either protecting commerce or attacking the enemy's shipping. These differences can be summarized:

The British compensated for their comparative lack of interest in the experimental side of naval architecture by devoting considerable resources to determining the sailing qualities of individual ships. No two ships of the same design were ever exactly alike. Information on changes to rig and ballasting made by one captain were not only recorded but passed on to his successor in the form of advice which he could ignore or alter if he chose. The Navy Board's surveyors were often able to re-rig a French prize to improve its sailing qualities, and if a captain subsequently found that a modification to that rig improved her sailing it was recorded. What also emerges from Navy Board reports is that the light scantlings of French ships made them more expensive to maintain than English-built ships, and many prizes spent an inordinate time in the dockyards.

There were more human factors in the constant harping on the superiority of French ships. The Royal Navy had a professional officer corps, which had no right to purchase its rank, and as it was predominantly recruited from comparatively poor younger sons (traditionally, if he was to make a career, the oldest son went into the Army unless there was a very strong naval connection) they were expected to reap their financial rewards from prize-money. The payment of a cash award based on the value of a captured ship was

French	British
1. Light construction	1. Robust construction
2. Very high speed in ideal conditions, usually at one particular point of sailing	2. All-round seakeeping, especially in rough weather
3. Less stability at large angles of heel, reducing their ability to carry canvas in high winds	3. High reserve of stability, giving a steady gun-platform and enabling sail to be carried in all weathers
4. Sailing better in light conditions and able to 'ghost' in light airs	4. Reasonable average speed on all points of sailing
5. Less firepower than English frigates	5. Heavier armament than French ships of similar dimensions

Right: Rowlandson's view of the rascally Purser, 1800.
Far right: His view of the Cook's Mate, usually a mutilated veteran incapable of normal duties.

nominal broadside of twenty 24-pounders, for example, was vastly superior to the same number of 18-pounders. What confused the issue even further was the 'rating' of ships by the number of guns; it was a nominal figure, and by the third quarter of the century many additional guns, particularly the short-ranged carronades, were carried but not included in the nominal total.

Thanks to the work done by the Navy Board in providing sound ships, and to the seamanship and experience of the officers and men, and in spite of the crippling restrictions of the Permanent Fighting Instructions, the Royal Navy was to find new laurels in the Seven Years' War with France.

British sailors swarm aboard a French
warship during a 'cutting out' expedition.

The Seven Years War

What makes the Seven Years' War so fascinating to modern historians is the way in which a series of naval disasters was redeemed by the determination of one man to make use of a maritime strategy. For the first time since the Elizabethans, there was a clear vision of the large-scale strategic gains to be made by sending the Royal Navy into distant waters, as opposed to disputing possession of the waters around the British Isles. It is for that reason that naval historians give William Pitt the Elder such a high place in the pantheon of sea power. He was in effect the first apostle of 'Blue Water' seapower.

As so often happens the war started disastrously. The French acted rapidly in the Mediterranean, sending an expedition to capture the island of Minorca in the Balearics, for they knew that possession of the fine natural harbour of Port Mahon and the fortress of St Philip was essential to the Royal Navy if it wished to blockade Toulon. The French force landed on Minorca, and belatedly the Honourable John Byng was sent with ten warships and a number of troops to relieve the garrison. As already mentioned, Byng was not able to get past a French squadron under la Galissonière, and because he seems to have been obsessed with the need to keep his line of battle intact, he failed to outwit the French. Even so the situation might have been retrieved, but Byng was not a resolute man, and he accepted the verdict of his captains the next day that he should abandon all attempts to relieve Minorca. By 14th June 1756 the British squadron was back in Gibraltar, and ten days after that General Blakeney was forced to surrender the fortress of St Philip to the French. As we know, Byng was chosen to be the scapegoat, but King George and his ministers must have known that their dilatoriness was as much to blame for the disaster as Byng.

In the Far East things went considerably better, for the British had the brilliant Robert Clive operating on land against the French and their Indian allies. Clive was lucky to have intelligent naval colleagues in Rear-Admirals Charles Watson and George Pocock. When Clive wished to recapture Calcutta Watson used his ships to give maximum support. Pocock then joined Watson in a brilliant attack on Chandernagore, 50 miles up the Hooghly River above Calcutta. By securing the river and the port of Calcutta the Navy thus ensured that Clive could win his decisive victory at Plassey the following year.

By 1760 France's attempts to establish a trading empire in India had been defeated, thanks largely to Clive's brilliance on land, but none of it would have been possible without the support of the Navy. Pocock fought three hard battles with the French ships in 1758-59, and was able to frustrate French attempts to take Madras.

The lessons of India were not lost on William Pitt, and when he came to power as Prime Minister he was determined to make better use of the Royal Navy against France, which had now added Corsica to her gains in the Mediterranean. To distract the enemy's attention he ordered a series of pinprick raids on the French coast, while the main strength of the Royal Navy was used to convoy General Amherst's 12,000 soldiers across the Atlantic. Their purpose was to attack French possessions in Canada, and after Cape Breton fell a second expedition under General Wolfe was sent to attack Quebec.

Once again the success on land was underwritten by the Navy. Wolfe was a talented, imaginative but erratic general, and he was lucky that Rear-Admiral Saunders had a temperament which

Right above: East Indiamen by Pocock.

Below: Capture of Chandernagore in March 1757.

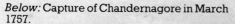

counterbalanced his self-doubt. Saunders also had the benefit of a brilliant navigator, James Cook, who surveyed the St Lawrence River with meticulous accuracy. The troops were taken up the river in ships' boats, the sailors using muffled oars to hide their presence from French sentries. After a long climb up to the Heights of Abraham the troops scored a sharp victory over the French, and although both commanding generals were killed the future of Canada had been decided. It remained only to secure the surrender of Montreal in September 1760 to bring French rule in North America to an end.

Pitt knew full well that these brilliant victories would be very quickly wiped out if France could send reinforcements of men and ships abroad, and that it was essential to beat the French Navy in Europe to safeguard the achievements overseas. Admiral Boscawen, on his return from the capture of Cape Breton, was sent to the Mediterranean to prevent the Toulon Fleet from getting through the Straits of Gibraltar to join up with the Brest

Above: HMS *Royal William* carried General Wolfe's body back to England after the capture of Quebec.

Left: Sir Edward Hawke's squadron moving into Quiberon Bay.
Below: View of Cape Rouge, nine miles above Quebec, on the North shore. From here about 1500 troops went downriver, on 13th September, 1759, to attack the French.

Fleet. The British public, cheated for so long of impressive victories at sea, were overjoyed to learn that Boscawen had trounced de la Clue in the Battle of Lagos on 18th August 1759, followed by Hawke's defeat of de Conflans at Quiberon Bay just three months later. What made Hawke's victory all the more important was his willingness to ignore the Permanent Fighting Instructions. It was the beginning of a new attitude to tactics, a reaffirmation of that tradition of victory which had started in 1588.

Hawke's squadron was lying off Brest, watching the main French fleet in its magnificent harbour and making sure that it did not get out to mount a long-awaited invasion of England. Lying off the coast of north Brittany required seamanship and leadership of the highest order. Not only were the ships exposed to the full fury of the Atlantic gales but the men were forced to endure the monotony of months on end of foul weather and the misery of cramped quarters and bad food. It was bad weather which brought on the battle, for a westerly gale had forced Hawke to fall back on Torbay, and allowed de Conflans to sail. As soon as he learned of the escape of the Brest squadron (21 ships of the line as against his own 23) Hawke proceeded in hot pursuit. Conflans decided to take shelter in Quiberon Bay, hoping that its shoals and strong tides would deter his pursuers.

He reckoned without Hawke, who sent his ships among the shoals to seek out the enemy. The rout was complete, for there was no escape. Nor was there time to organize a defence, for as Conflans was bringing the head of his squadron into the bay his rearguard was under attack. The 74-gun ship *Formidable*, flagship of Rear-

Admiral Verger, and the *Héros* were cut off, and had to surrender after sustaining heavy damage. The risks taken by Hawke were considerable, and he saw both the *Essex* and *Resolution* wrecked on the shoals of Quiberon Bay before victory was certain. When darkness fell the flagship *Royal George* signalled to the fleet to anchor, but there was one more ship to add to the score. At first light next morning lookouts sighted a large ship lying at anchor, dismasted. It was the French flagship herself, the *Soleil Royal*, but before the British ships could attack her she was deliberately run aground.

What distinguished Hawke's victory was its completeness. For the first time since the Dutch Wars, nearly a century earlier, a British admiral had gained a clear-cut and decisive victory. Over half of the French squadron had been captured or destroyed, 11 out of 21, and the remainder were nearly all hiding in the mouth of the river Vilaine, where they were forced to stay for two years. It was the end of another scheme for the invasion of England, and it reaffirmed the success of the blockade. The French were forced to give up for the moment any idea of disputing the possession of the seas, and fell back on privateering as the only means of waging war. It was the age of the *corsairs* like Jean Bart, who operated out of Dunkirk, St Malo and other small harbours.

Neither the death of George II in October 1760 nor the intervention of Spain on the side of France was able to deflect Pitt from his grand strategy, and with the new confidence gained by the Royal Navy there was little reason to fear even the combined fleets of France and Spain. It is no coincidence that Hawke's subordinates included such future flag-officers as Howe, Keppel and Rodney, and it seemed that at last the baleful influence of party politics had been eradicated.

George Rodney, now a Rear-Admiral, was appointed to command an expedition to the West Indies. Led by the flagship *Marlborough* (74 guns), the squadron sailed from Spithead on 18th October 1761 and arrived off Martinique three months later. The siege of Fort Royal was conducted with vigour, and by the beginning of February the whole island was in British hands. Once Martinique was secure the capture of the smaller islands Grenada, St Lucia and St Vincent was simple, and a bigger expedition against the Spanish possessions could be planned.

The expedition to capture Havana achieved a remarkable standard of co-ordination between the Royal Navy and the British Army, one which was not to be repeated for many years. Admiral Pocock was appointed to command the naval forces, 19 ships of the line and a number of frigates, and the Earl of Albemarle had 10,000 troops. The Spanish made little attempt to stop the assembly of the ex-

Above: Sir Edward Hawke, first of a new breed of admirals willing to achieve outright victory, even at the risk of ignoring the Fighting Instructions.

pedition, and when Pocock's squadron arrived off Havana 12 warships and a large number of merchantmen were still lying at anchor under the guns of Morro Castle. By a clever feint the British succeeded in capturing the castle, giving them the command of the anchorage, but it still took another 53 days of siege warfare before Havana fell. The treasure captured was immense, and Pocock and Albemarle

Above: Indiamen at sea in a light breeze. These large merchantmen were doughty antagonists for most privateers.

Below: The Battle of Quiberon Bay on 20 November, 1759 was proof that Hawke's methods would recreate the tradition of victory.

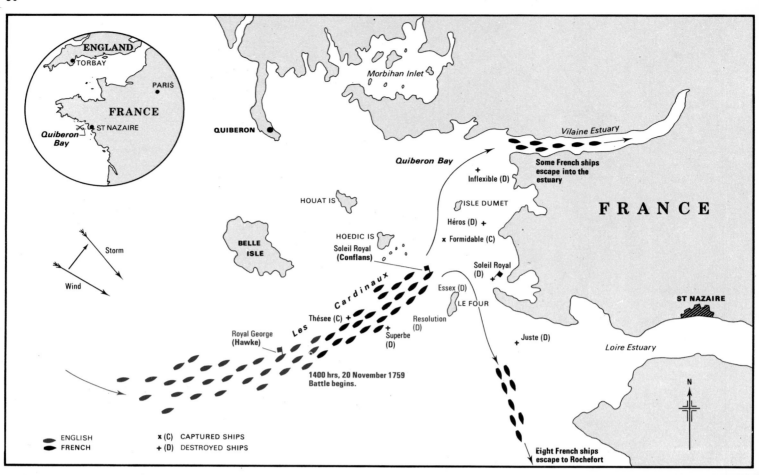

ENGLAND
TORBAY
PARIS
FRANCE
ST NAZAIRE
Quiberon
Bay

Morbihan Inlet

QUIBERON

Vilaine Estuary

Quiberon Bay

Some French ships
escape into the
estuary

+ Inflexible (D)

ISLE DUMET

HOUAT IS

Héros (D) +

x Formidable (C)

FRANCE

Storm

HOEDIC IS

Wind

Soleil Royal
(Conflans)

Soleil Royal
(D)

ST NAZAIRE

Les Cardinaux

Essex (D)

LE FOUR

Thésee (C) +

Resolution
(D)

Royal George
(Hawke)

+ Superbe
(D)

+ Juste (D)

Loire Estuary

1400 hrs, 20 November 1759
Battle begins.

N

ENGLISH
FRENCH

x (C) CAPTURED SHIPS
+ (D) DESTROYED SHIPS

Eight French ships
escape to Rochefort

each received £120,000 as his share of the prize-money.

The long arm of sea power was able to chastise Spain in the Pacific as well. On 23rd September 1762 a Royal Navy squadron under Admiral Cornish dropped anchor off Cavite near Manila in the Philippines. With only 2000 troops available Cornish was forced to land an additional 900 sailors and marines, but once again boldness won the day, and on 6th October the Spanish Governor capitulated.

The combined effect of these hammer blows, the destruction of the main French Fleet at Quiberon Bay and the loss of Spain's most important overseas possessions, forced both countries to sue for peace. By the Treaty of Paris concluded in February 1763 France was forced to yield all claims to Canada, Nova Scotia and Cape Breton, but in return was allowed to keep Guadeloupe and Martinique, and gained the islands of St Pierre and

Above right: The celebrated mutiny aboard HMS *Bounty*. Captain Bligh and those loyal to him are cast adrift to begin their epic voyage to Timor.

Below left: Three sail-of-the-line attacking Morro Castle during the siege of Havana in 1762.

Miquelon off the coast of Canada. Spain regained control of Havana and Manila, but not Minorca. Although critics maintained that Pitt would have driven a harder bargain had he still been in office, the terms were hardly favourable to the vanquished. Much of what was to become the British Empire was gained during the Seven Years' War, and above all it showed the British just what benefits could be gained from the adroit use of sea power. Not since the Dutch Wars had the Navy won such handsome gains for the Nation.

It is worth asking just what combination of factors made the Seven Years' War so successful. We have already seen that the design of British ships had reached a new standard of excellence, but that could not alone account for the dazzling victories. More important was the continuity of good administration provided by Lord Anson as First Lord of the Admiralty. With only short interruptions he held the office from 1751 until his death in 1762, and he fully deserves the credit given him by later generations. The Royal Navy needed reform badly, and Anson had the additional virtue of being able to work well with William Pitt.

The great work done by Anson was not thrown away, for in 1766 Pitt, now raised to the peerage as Lord Chatham, offered Admiral Boscawen the job of First Lord of the Admiralty. Under his tutelage officers of ability were allowed to develop their talents, and this 'seed corn' was to tide the Navy over in the American War.

The early death of Boscawen at the age of 50 robbed the Navy of a brilliant officer, who might have gone on to do even more. Known as 'Old Dreadnought' he was credited with having appeared on the quarterdeck in his nightshirt. When the officer of the watch reported two French ships and asked what to do, Boscawen replied 'Do? Do, dammit? Fight 'em!'

The end of the fighting enabled scientific and exploration work to continue in the distant seas. It was an age of rapid scientific advance, and it is to the credit of the Royal Navy that it rendered invaluable assistance to the discoverers. That same James Cook who had surveyed the St Lawrence for Admiral Saunders before the capture of Quebec became Marine Surveyor of Newfoundland, producing a series of charts of lasting value to trade and safety at sea. In 1769 Cook was appointed to command the *Endeavour* and to take her to the Pacific to observe the Transit of Venus. It is often stated that no-one of humble birth could rise in the 18th century Royal Navy, but the rise to fame of Cook, once the skipper of a Whitby collier, proves that this is at best a generalization. After his return in 1771 he was given command of another expedition, and from 1772 to 1775 he voyaged around the world, charting unknown seas and discovering new lands.

Cook's second voyage was remarkable for the good health of his men. He followed the recommendations of James Lind, a doctor who recommended the use of fresh vegetables and lemon juice as a counter to scurvy, and for his careful attention to diet and health he was awarded the gold medal of the Royal Society. Details have survived of 18th century diet, and we know that in 1720 the allowance was:

Biscuit	– 16 ounces per day
Lean Salt Beef	– 32 ounces twice weekly
Salt Pork	– 16 ounces twice weekly
Pease	– 8 ounces four days per week
Dried Fish	– 2 ounces three days per week
Butter	– 2 ounces three days per week
Cheese	– 4 ounces three days per week
Beer	– 1 gallon per day

Above: In the destruction of French power in the West Indies the capture of Martinique was followed by St Lucia and Grenada.

It has been calculated that this would provide a seaman with 4450 calories per day, and would give him enough energy, but in the words of a modern authority it was 'unpalatable and nutritionally disastrous.' Salt remained the principal means of preserving food until well into the 19th century, but it was uncertain, and there could be no guarantee that the recommended scale of rations listed above would be feasible after a few weeks at sea.

Even allowing for the natural decay of rations, the stores taken on board were not always as fresh as the victualling yard liked to believe. Pepys had made great efforts to stamp out corruption among the Navy's contractors, but provisions were usually underweight, incompletely pre-

served or even in an advanced state of decay. William Thompson's pamphlet of 1761 paints a horrifying picture: 'The bread, so full of large black maggots that the men . . . be obliged to shut their eyes to confine that sense from being offended before they could bring their minds into the resolution of consuming it . . . the beer has stunk as abominably as the foul stagnant water which is pumped out of many cellars of London . . .' As if this was not bad enough the system was administered by pursers, who were expected to make a profit. They were entitled to deduct an eighth of the value of everything supplied to the men to allow for unavoidable wastage, and given the wide prevalence of illiteracy, a dishonest man had ample scope for fraud.

The man who did most to improve the sailor's lot was James Lind, a Scot who studied surgery in Edinburgh. He entered the Royal Navy as a Surgeon's Mate in 1739

and in 1747 was appointed to the 4th Rate HMS *Salisbury*. Lind was deeply distressed by the circumnavigation of the world by Admiral Anson, in which scurvy and other diseases had accounted for no fewer than 1051 out of the 1955 men embarked. He began a careful study of scurvy and in 1747 began a controlled experiment with 12 seamen. Dividing them into six pairs, he fed each pair of scurvy patients a different remedy, ranging from cider, diluted sulphuric acid, vinegar, and oranges and lemons, to a mixture of garlic and mustard seeds. Only cider showed anything like the miraculous effect of the cirtus fruit, for at the end of only six days two of his patients were fit to return to duty while the others were worse.

It took another 40 years for Lind's find-

Below: Pocock's capture of Havana in 1762 was a bold and imaginative stroke. Navy and Army each played their part in achieving success.

mighty forests of English oak were already being thinned out, and there was a growing tendency to rely on North American timber.

The ships were built with the simplest tools, the axe, two-handed saw, adze and auger, used by shipwrights in the same manner as they had been in the Middle Ages. By the 1770s iron fastenings were common, in addition to large wooden pegs known as 'treenails' or 'trennels.' The first part of the ship to be built was the keel, followed by the stem and stern pieces, made of specially chosen, naturally curved 'compass timbers.' Then the frames were set up, about a foot apart, performing much the same function as the rib-cage in the human body. When time permitted the hull was left to stand 'in frame' so that the timber could season. In time of emergency ships were often built of 'green' or unseasoned wood, and they succumbed to dry rot, whereas 'well-found' ships lasted for 30 years or more.

The masting and rigging of a man o' war required the same sort of specialized skill as the building of the hull. That complicated mass of ropes and spars was in fact a complex machine which extracted power from the wind and supported the tall masts. The standing rigging and running rigging would all be fitted by riggers, using ropes woven in covered ropewalks. The larger warships were all three-masted with square sail on each mast, a rig known simply as 'ship rig.' There were, however, additional fore-and-aft sails. Below the rank of frigate, rigs became more diverse, with ship-rigged sloops, single-masted cutters and schooners.

There was also the confusing matter of rates. Any ship-rigged warship of 20 guns or more was graded in a system of six

Below: Captain James Cook rose from captain of a Whitby collier to become a leading scientific figure whose improvements in navigation transformed the very nature of seapower.

ings to be fully accepted by the Admiralty, but in the meantime enlightened captains like James Cook followed his recommendations, and the ideas gradually spread throughout the Navy. Although the West Indian lime has become associated with antiscorbutic medicine, and Royal Navy sailors were known in the 19th century as 'Limeys', the fruit adopted was the Sicilian lime, a species of lemon; no wonder captains like Cook sometimes had to enforce the drinking of a pint of lemon juice with the threat of a flogging. Admiral Rodney's Physician of the Fleet, Sir Gilbert Blane, finally persuaded his superiors to put Lind's precepts to the test, and when he was appointed Commissioner for the Sick and Hurt Board advised the Board to authorize the issue of lemon juice and fruit on demand. It was 1795, one year after the death of James Lind.

It is often thought that surgery in the 18th century was primitive in the extreme. Amputations may have been done without anaesthetics but in complete contrast the treatment for burns would have done credit to more modern burns units. Following the publication of Benjamin Gooch's *Chirurgical Works* in 1767 naval surgeons began to treat burns scientifically to avoid fusion of scar tissue and loss of movement in the hands. Tradition has it that naval surgeons were drunken incompetents who operated with a cheerful disregard for the patient's suffering but the facts reflect a rather different picture.

By the end of the Seven Years' War the Royal Navy was made up of a series of standard types of ship, built by methods which were standard throughout Europe and North America. Oak remained the most popular material, for it was available in large quantities, but elm was also used and decks were usually planked with fir. Large quantities were needed, as many as 5700 cartloads of wood for a 1st Rate. The

Above left: Model of the 70-gun ship *Ipswich* of 1730, typical of contemporary Admiralty Board models built to demonstrate details of new designs.

Above right: On 20th February, 1758 HMS *Monmouth* (64 guns) captured the French *Foudroyant*, while *Revenge* and *Berwick* captured the *Orphee*, and *Monarch* and *Montagu* drove the *Oriflamme* ashore.

'rates,' starting with 1st Rates (100 guns or more) and proceeding downwards through 2nd Rates (90-98 guns), 3rd Rates (64-84 guns), 4th Rates (50-60 guns), 5th rates (28-44 guns) and 6th Rates (20-28 guns). The smaller ships were rated as frigates or 'post ships,' because they were the smallest ships fit to be commanded by a captain. The larger frigates fell into the category of 5th Rates and were intended to 'cruize' independently. Ranking below frigates were sloops of 8-20 guns, cutters, schooners, bombs (armed with mortars for shore bombardment), fireships and transports, among others. The difference between merchant ships and warships was not as marked as it is today, and in particular the 'East Indiamen' built by the Honourable East India Company for trade with India and the Far East were often as well-armed as warships. There were also West Indiamen and a host of small mercantile types such as collier barks, hoys and feluccas.

Naval gunnery had advanced considerably by the middle of the 18th century. For at least a hundred years the 'truck carriage' gun mounting had been standard, a simple wooden base for the gun, on four solid wooden wheels. The gun was cast of bronze or iron (brass was also used, but only for small guns) with projections on either side, known as trunnions. The gun was secured to the 'cheeks' of the carriage by dropping the trunnions into depressions cut into the wood, and two 'cap-squares' then locked them in place. The gun was operated by a series of ropes and pulleys, which could run it up to the hinged port in the ship's side, or it could be traversed from side to side with the help of crowbar-like implements called handspikes. Elevating or depressing the gun was done by means of moving a 'quoin' or wedge in or out from under the breech end of the barrel, and loading was done from the muzzle end, as breech-loading had disappeared after the Elizabethan period. When the gun was run back 'inboard' a bagged cartridge of gunpowder was pushed to the back of the barrel, followed by a wad of felt, then the round cast iron shot, sometimes followed by another felt wad to stop the 'roundshot' from rolling out.

Once the gun was loaded one of the guncrew used a spike known as a 'pricker' thrust down the touch-hole to pierce the powder cartridge inside the gun, and then sprinkled a dash of powder into the touch-hole, using a powder horn carried on his belt. The gun was then run out by the guncrew hauling on the ropes, and the 'captain of the gun,' the senior member of the crew, took a slow match from a tub lying on the deck, and pushed it

Below: The 3rd Rate *Magnificent* (74 guns) was wrecked near Brest on 25 March, 1804.

into the touch-hole to set fire to the loose gunpowder lying there. The gun then fired and flung itself backwards, sometimes on its trucks but often rising clear of the deck, and was only checked from running right across the deck by thick rope 'breechings' fastened to the side timbers. In all it took up to 15 men (depending on the size of gun) to accomplish this process, although in an emergency fewer men could still operate the gun. The British preferred to hit an enemy ship 'between wind and water', in other words on the hull, whereas the French fired high (on the upward roll) to disable rigging. But above all British training emphasized rapidity and accuracy of firing. Contrary to popular belief the guns of the 18th century could range up to two miles (3500 yards) but there was little chance of hitting anything at such 'random' ranges, and a good gunner was unlikely to get a hit at more than a mile. The average gunner was best at ranges of quarter of a mile or less, and close range action became fashionable. The ideal was the massive 'broadside' but this had the disadvantage of straining the ship's timbers. Repeated broadsides had a crushing moral effect but they could not be kept up for long, even by the fittest crews, and they soon gave way to 'ripple' firing, in which each gun on the gun deck fired in quick succession.

The largest gun afloat in the Royal Navy at this time was the 42-pounder, which fired a cannonball weighing 42 pounds (roughly 7 inches in calibre) but it was not popular because it was a heavy and cumbersome gun. The handier 32-pounder, firing a 6.3-inch shot, was to become the most popular and successful, but there were also 24-, 18-, 12-, 9- and 6-pounders. Small merchant ships were armed with 4- and 3-pounders, and the bombs were armed with 10-inch or 13-inch mortars, the only example of guns rated by calibre. There were also small anti-personnel weapons known as 'swivels.' They were normally mounted on forked supports rotating in slots in the gunwales, or in the fighting tops (platforms at various levels on the masts). They were the lineal descendants of the 'murderers' in Elizabethan times, and were mainly used to repel boarding parties.

Sailors were armed with a variety of weapons for hand-to-hand fighting; principally the cutlass, supplemented by pistols and muskets, tomahawks, pikes, hatchets or any other unpleasant weapon that came to hand. Despite the dominance of the ship-gun a wooden ship could take a surprising amount of pounding without sinking, and boarding was still the normal way to finish an action. To hamper attempts to board, a man o' war went into action with 'boarding nets' triced up across the upper deck, and guncrews were issued with boarding pikes, six-foot steel-tipped poles used to spear boarders as they tried to hack their way through the boarding nets. The shout of 'Stand by to repel boarders' was a signal to the upper deck guncrews to drop their rammers, sponges or handspikes, seize whatever weapons were handy and charge headlong into the fray. Equally, the seamen had to be ready for the moment when their officers judged that any enemy's fire had slackened sufficiently to indicate that a large percentage of her crew had been killed or injured. Then the order 'Boarding parties away' was the signal for a mad onslaught over the enemy's bulwarks. These actions were usually brief but bloody affairs, and contemporary descriptions of scuppers running with blood were probably not exaggerated.

This then in broad outline was the state of naval warfare at the end of the Seven Years' War. Not totally haphazard but not

Above: HMS *Ramillies* was a 3rd Rate 74-gun ship built at Chatham in 1763. She was damaged in a hurricane off the Newfoundland Banks and then caught fire, on 16 September, 1782.

Right: A British squadron off Goree in September 1758.

Left: HMS *Centaur* (74 guns) was the French *Centaure*, captured on 18 August, 1759 at Lagos. She was lost off the Grand Banks in September 1782.

yet subject to the influences of industrial power. And yet the Royal Navy was about to reap the the benefits of Britain's Industrial Revolution. What the 20th century knows as 'quality control' was in its infancy, but the introduction of standard weights and measures gave Great Britain an advantage over her European neighbours. No longer would a powder charge made in Scotland differ slightly in weight from one made in the south of England. The mighty Admiralty machine had become, after government itself, the biggest spender in the country, and as an industrial concern in its own right it was bound to be affected by the pace of industrial change in civilian life.

The Battle of Frigate Bay in January 1782.

War Against Kith and Kin

To the Americans it was the War of Independence, to the British it was known simply as the American War, the war fought between Great Britain and her rebellious American colonies from 1775 to 1783. But in fact it came close to being a world war, at least by 18th century standards. By the end every European country was hostile to Britain, and even those who did not declare war had chosen to form themselves into a League of Armed Neutrality, threatening the naval stores which were vital to the Navy.

The origins of the war are well known – growing American irritation at British restraints on trade, and the various taxes on commodities. Add to that the smouldering hostility of France, and a local insurrection was turned into a major war. At first it was no more than a local insurrection, for although the official proclamation declaring that the colonies were in a state of rebellion was published in 1775 serious military operations to counteract it did not begin until after the Declaration of Independence the following July.

This is not to say that nothing of any significance happened in the first months. Far from it, for the Continental Congress lost no time in issuing Letters of Marque, and the individual States did likewise. The cheap timber of New England had already been exploited to build excellent ships, and by 1774 about one-third of British merchant ships were built in Canada and America. New England also bred proficient deep-water sailors, and during the Seven Years' War and earlier wars Americans had proved adept at commerce-raiding. Before the first shots of Lexington had died away patriotic merchants started to fit out privateers, and indeed so many sailors and shipwrights became involved in these preparations that Congress and the States had difficulty in recruiting men and building ships for the regular navies. Inevitably, therefore, the fledgling naval forces of the colonies were mainly dedicated to commerce-raiding as well. By 1776 there were over 130 American privateers operating, and by 1781 the number had risen to 449; these ships carried up to 15 guns and before the end of hostilities had captured over 600 British vessels.

The individual States' navies also took part in commerce-raiding but also devoted some of their resources to coast defence. The ships used for this purpose tended to be small gunboats, galleys or even floating batteries. The biggest was the Navy of Massachusetts, followed by the Navy of Virginia. Their efforts at coast defence were less successful than privateering, by and large. The so-called Continental Navy, in contrast, achieved very little. As early as October 1775 Congress bought 16 ships and appointed a Naval Committee but it proved exceptionally difficult to build up a disciplined and well-administered navy quickly.

When the British finally realized that they stood to lose their North American colonies the response was too little and too late. At first Vice-Admiral Lord Howe's forces had no difficulty in capturing New York, Rhode Island and Philadelphia. Canadian forces had little difficulty in repulsing a daring raid by Benedict Arnold, and the American forces fell back on Lake Champlain in headlong retreat. Only the brilliant leadership of Arnold prevented the British from seizing the initiative, for he at once set about building a small fleet to defend Lake Champlain.

The British did not know that Benedict Arnold had cunningly hidden his galleys, schooners and gundalows between Valcour Island and the shore, and had sailed past before they saw the Americans. They were caught on the wrong foot, forced to beat back against the wind, and as a result some of their most powerful ships took a long time to get into action. Eventually the weight of fire began to tell, and by nightfall the American forces had to admit defeat, escaping under cover of darkness. But Arnold had done what he intended, to delay the arrival of British reinforcements

Above: The 44-gun *Serapis* was beaten by the *Bonhomme Richard*, a converted French Indiaman commanded by John Paul Jones.

Top right: The brig *Lexington*, one of a number of ships which formed the Continental Navy of 1776.

Right: Destruction of American shipping at Penobscot Bay.

from Canada; the surrender of General Burgoyne at Saratoga the following year was the direct outcome.

Burgoyne's surrender at Saratoga in October 1777 changed the whole character of the war for it persuaded France that her moment had come to recover Canada and to inflict lasting damage on her traditional enemy. Her recognition of the United States and the signing of a treaty between the new republic and France was calculated to annoy the British, and war followed quickly. Just before the breach finally occurred there was an extraordinary action between two frigates off Plouescat, in Brittany. A British squadron under Vice-Admiral the Honourable Augustus Keppel was cruis-

ing off Brest when lookouts sighted the French 30-gun frigate *La Belle Poule*. The French ship, commanded by Isaac de la Clocheterie, had put out from Brest in June 1778, and she closed with Keppel's 20-strong force with the obvious intention of counting heads and reporting on the squadron's course. Anglo-French relations were so close to breaking point that several British frigates, including the fast 32-gun *Arethusa*, took off in hot pursuit. After an exchange of insults gunfire followed, and the result was a five-hour engagement.

The cutter *Alert* captured the lugger *Coureur*, leaving the two frigates to battle it out. The English and French accounts are very hard to reconcile, for both sides regarded it as a victory. But the difference was that in France the action was hailed as a humiliation for the British, and it was said that the *Arethusa* had turned tail and fled from the *Belle Poule*. De la Clocheterie was rewarded by the King and a new fashion of hair styled *a la Belle Poule* was adopted at Court. Coming as it did fresh on the heels of Saratoga, and

following the assiduous diplomacy of Benjamin Franklin in Paris, it hardened French resolve to seize the opportunity to humiliate the British once and for all.

It was a propitious moment for the French. The losses of the previous war had been made good, the dockyard organization had been overhauled and much corruption had been purged by the energetic Navy Minister, the Duc de Choiseul. The very completeness of the defeat in the Seven Years' War had produced a burning desire for a naval renaissance. Money was provided by the Church, individual towns and the provinces, to buy new ships, and in 1778 there were 80 ships-of-the-line, as against only 35 in 1758. The Marine Academy founded at Brest in 1752 was turning out officers generally recognized as being the best-educated in Europe. In the theory of their profession, at least, the French officer corps was second to none, and naval architects like Sané were also respected by their contemporaries. The Naval Decrees of 1765 had had a similar effect on the dockyard administration, and it can

Right: The 5th Rate HMS *Pearl* (32 guns) capturing the *Santa Monica* in 1779.

Far right: The Bailli de Suffren fought six hard battles against Sir Edward Hughes in the Indian Ocean.

Below: The Battle of Negapatam on 6 July, 1782, between Hughes and Suffren.

The action between the *Serapis* and the
Bonhomme Richard.

Top right: The 5th Rate 32-gun *Quebec* blew up after action with the French *Surveillante* off Ushant on 6 October, 1779.

Above: Rodney's action at St Vincent in the West Indies on 16 January, 1780, sometimes known as the 'Moonlight Battle'.

Left: The Battle of the Saints, 1782.

Below: In the Battle of the Saints, Sir George Rodney beat and captured Comte de Grasse, victor at the Chesapeake.

be said that the French Navy was well placed to defeat the Royal Navy.

The Royal Navy was not in ideal shape after a long period of peace. The inevitable cutback in expenditure had taken its toll of dockyard efficiency, and it was reputed that the indolent First Lord of the Admiralty, the Earl of Sandwich, had allowed grass to grow on the decks of the ships laid up in Ordinary. But time was to show that some of the worst insults thrown at Sandwich's head by his political rivals (he was known as 'Jemmy Twitcher') were undeserved, for his apparently ramshackle organization held up surprisingly well under the strain of war. The French organization, in contrast, looked imposing but had certain deeprooted flaws.

The main problem in the French Navy was the undue influence of aristocratic connections; it was much harder for a junior officer in the Royal Navy to quarrel with a superior officer for the Royal Navy paid great attention to the hierarchy of rank. There were very few instances of sprigs of the nobility being able to dictate to grizzled captains, for each captain and

admiral had his place in order of seniority. Another difficulty in the French Navy was the obsession with theoretical pursuit of the 'objective,' a tactical or strategic aim which was always held to be of overriding importance. On many occasions a French squadron held off from clinching a victory over an inferior British force, in order to preserve the ships for some purpose.

The combination of American daring and French sea power nonetheless put the Royal Navy under the most severe pressure. The Continental Navy's sloop *Ranger*, under the command of John Paul Jones, raided the English coast and captured the 20-gun sloop *Drake*. Fortunately for the British an attempt to build 74-gun 3rd Rates was unsuccessful, but the French supplied frigates and lesser warships. With men like Jones even the worst ships could achieve much, as he showed when given command of a dilapidated East Indiaman called the *Duc de Duras*. Under her new name *Bonhomme Richard* Jones began a career of destruction which caused the British great consternation; to them he was a pirate, but to the Americans he was their first naval hero. On 25th September 1779 he fell in with a convoy off Flamborough Head, escorted by the 44-gun ship HMS *Serapis* and a sloop.

The battle which followed was one of those bloody actions in which neither side is prepared to admit defeat. The captain of the *Serapis*, Richard Pearson, had the advantage in gunpower and initially succeeded in silencing the lower deck of the *Bonhomme Richard*. But eventually the French marines lent to Jones, and seamen in the fighting tops, succeeded in dropping a grenade down on to the deck of the *Serapis*, where it detonated a number of powder cartridges. The *Serapis* surrendered but the *Bonhomme Richard* was so sorely battered that she was later abandoned – only the iron will of John Paul Jones had kept her in the fight.

The entry of France into the war brought about the first fleet action quite soon. On 27th July 1778 Keppel met d'Orvilliers off Ushant, after four days of sparring to secure the 'weather gauge.' When the direction of the wind finally changed Keppel succeeded in crossing in the wake of the French and attacked their rearguard. The British wanted to close the range while the French intended to keep as far away as possible, and a disagreement between Keppel and his second-in-command, Palliser, made it even harder than usual to get to grips with the enemy. Finally after a cannonade as the ships passed one another in succession the French drew out of range. They had lost more men (163 killed and 573 wounded, as against 133 British killed and 375 wounded) but they had cut up the British ships' rigging severely. But true to his higher objective, d'Orvilliers made no attempt to destroy Keppel and tamely returned to Brest. It was this action which led to the shabby attempt to indict Keppel for not following the Fighting Instructions, but it was the last gasp of the old system of political interference in naval affairs.

After the Battle of Ushant the emphasis shifted from European waters to the other side of the Atlantic. The first French fleet to arrive was a squadron of 11 sail of the line under the Comte d'Estaing. It fought an inconclusive engagement off Rhode Island in August 1778 and then made a brief foray into the Caribbean before returning to France.

A second squadron under Admiral Destouches arrived two years later, bringing General Rochambeau and important reinforcements for General Washington. Once again, however, it was not handled with sufficient determination to break through the British Fleet. Third time was lucky for the French, however, for in August 1781, in response to urgent requests from Washington and Rochambeau, the West Indies squadron of Admiral Comte de Grasse was sent north. Its 28 sail of the line had two objectives, the first to help the American Army to concentrate around the beleaguered fortress of Yorktown, the second to prevent the Royal Navy from relieving Yorktown. De Grasse was an energetic leader who lost no time in blockading the Chesapeake, and on 5th September he was able to prevent the British Admiral Graves from breaking through his line. The Battle of the Chesapeake (otherwise known as the Battle of the Virginia Capes) was tactically no more than a draw, but its strategic significance was overwhelming. Before the British could repair the damage to their spars and rigging de Grasse had been reinforced by the French Newport squadron, and with 36 French sail of the line barring the way, there was no hope of dislodging them. Lord Cornwallis and his troops had to be abandoned, and their surrender followed on 19th October. The collapse broke the will of the British Government to continue the war, and negotiations for peace began almost immediately. It was a humiliating defeat, but it was inevitable for the British were over-

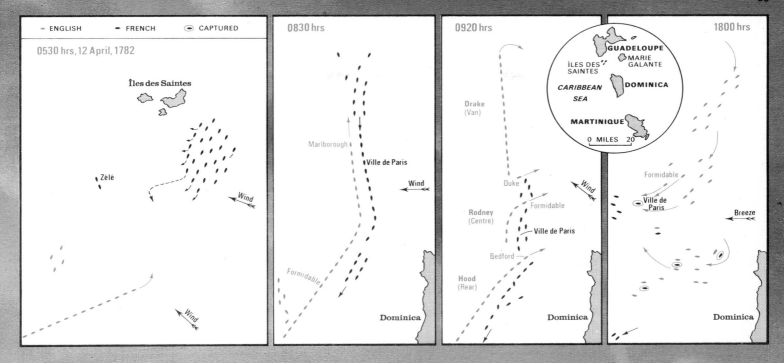

- ENGLISH   - FRENCH   ⊙ CAPTURED

0530 hrs, 12 April, 1782

Îles des Saintes

Zélé

Wind

Wind

0830 hrs

Marlborough

Ville de Paris

Wind

Formidable

Dominica

0920 hrs

Drake
(Van)

Duke

Rodney
(Centre)

Formidable

Ville de Paris

Bedford

Hood
(Rear)

Wind

Dominica

1800 hrs

GUADELOUPE

MARIE
GALANTE

ÎLES DES
SAINTES

DOMINICA

CARIBBEAN
SEA

MARTINIQUE

0 MILES 20

Formidable

Ville de
Paris

Breeze

Dominica

Below: Lord Howe's relief of Gibraltar on 11 October, 1782 saved the fortress at the eleventh hour.

Sir George Rodney, whose victory at the Saints rescued him from debt and obscurity.

extended. The Royal Navy was fighting the French in the Indian Ocean as well as the north and south Atlantic. Its vital supplies of cordage and tar, much of which came from Scandinavia, were threatened by the League of Armed Neutrality, and if Canada fell the Royal Navy would run out of timber. To try and guard all these sensitive areas and at the same time protect the home islands from invasion was more than the Royal Navy could manage on its own. Had the warnings of French expansion been heeded the Fleet might have been expanded, but the government had been content to bask in the reflected glory of the Seven Years' War and do as little as possible to maintain the Royal Navy.

Yet it was that same over-stretched Navy that saved the Government, showing that at bottom it was still a formidable fighting force. The scene was the West Indies, off a small group of islands known as the Saintes. There on 8th April 1782 the ailing Admiral Rodney caught de Grasse at a disadvantage, with only 31 ships of the line to match his own 37. The Frenchman had hoped to slip past Rodney's squadron to mount an attack on Jamaica, but the following day he decided to attack what was then the British van, commanded by Commodore Hood. During the next two days the British tried to get to grips with the French, and the French were gradually worn down because of damage sustained in the action against Hood. Finally on the evening of 11th April the two fleets were close enough for Rodney to form his line of battle, but he held off until daylight. Next morning Rodney got his chance, when a shift in the wind enabled him to take his flagship HMS *Formidable* through the French line. The *Formid-*

able's broadsides dismasted one French ship as she broke through, and it must have given considerable satisfaction to her captain, Howard Douglas, to think that Rodney had adopted his radical reforms in gunnery. There was no communications problem in this battle, for HMS *Duke* also cut through the French line, followed by the sixth ship astern of the *Formidable*, and eventually the whole of the British rearguard went through as well.

The formation of the French Fleet was totally shattered, and although many of them escaped five ships of the line and de Grasse himself fell into British hands. Although Hood would have dearly liked to pursue the fleeing French ships his Commander in Chief was content, saying 'Come, we have done very handsomely.' The real results of the Battle of the Saintes, however, could not be measured in terms of ships taken and prisoners captured. At the peace negotiations in Paris the French were dismayed by the news from the West Indies, and virtually abandoned their American allies to deal with the British by themselves. Until the news of Rodney's victory it had looked as if the British might lose Canada, but the Saintes changed that. In short the British were able to retrieve much from the debacle that they had no right to expect.

For the Royal Navy the American War had been a harrowing experience but nonetheless a useful one. Many weaknesses of training and tactics had been revealed, but when it is considered that the Royal Navy had faced the united navies of the United States, France, Spain and Holland, it had little to be ashamed of. The navies of Spain and Holland had been knocked out of the war with comparatively little trouble, and the reverses had been suffered at the hands of men who

Below: An 18-gun ordnance storeship running the blockade to get supplies into Gibraltar.

Above: Although Rodney was attacked by his subordinates for not capturing more ships at the Saints, his orders showed important tactical innovations.

were superlative captains. These reverses did much good to the Royal Navy, forcing a younger generation of officers to look closely at their system of training and command, and there can be no doubt that the harrowing years of 1776-1782 helped to shape the Royal Navy which won the Great War against France 10 years later.

Modern historians incline to the view that the financial strains imposed by the maximum effort of the American War opened the first of the cracks in the edifice of French monarchical power. Certainly in 1793 British captains commented that the fight appeared to have been knocked out of the French, and there is evidence to suggest that the French dockyard organ-

ization failed to meet the demands put upon it. In contrast the British dockyards rose magnificently to the occasion and refitted a much greater number of ships. More important, they were able to cope with an important technological change, coppering of ships' bottoms. By plating each ship's bottom timbers with thin copper sheeting it was possible to defeat the ship-worm, *teredo navalis*, and to prevent the accumulation of marine growths. This in turn meant that ships could maintain maximum speed for up to six months out of dock, an important advantage when fighting far from home.

The Royal Navy also introduced the carronade, its 'secret weapon.' This was a short-barrelled, large-calibre gun intended for close-range action. Because of its destructive effect against ship-timbers it was first known as a 'smasher' but was named the carronade after the Carron Foundry in Scotland where it was developed. In several actions carronades gave British ships an important advantage, and the French learned to stay out of range, rather than face them.

The most important lesson for the Royal Navy was that sea power must not be tied to supporting a land campaign, unless there are finite limits on the land operations. It has been said by modern American scholars that only the Royal Navy could have even contemplated a war in North America. Certainly without the Royal Navy's immense exertions the land war would have petered out sooner. Equally, if the Royal Navy had not been neglected in peacetime it would have been better able to deal with the French threat, and the Revolutionary Army under Washington might have been worn down. These are the might-have-beens of history, but they bear consideration.

Left: One of the famous Gibraltar mountings, which allowed a 24-pounder gun to fire downhill.

The climax of the Battle of the Nile in 1798, when the French flagship *l'Orient* blew up.

Dawn of
the Golden Age

The Royal Navy was exhausted after its exertions during the American War, and as the French seemed equally willing to lick their wounds an uneasy peace intervened. It lasted for ten years, even surviving the outbreak of revolution in France in 1789. Not until King Louis XVI was guillotined in January 1793 did the British Government feel willing to go to war against Republicanism, but in the event the National Convention precipitated hostilities by declaring war on Britain and Holland on 1st February.

The Royal Navy was outwardly in poor shape, having dropped from 100,000 sailors and marines in 1782 down to 20,000 at the time of the Revolution. But, whereas France's economic power was stagnating in the last decade of Bourbon power the British were in the throes of the Industrial Revolution. All the underlying advantages already noted, such as standard weights and measures, improved standards of manufacture and above all, efficient transport, were making Britain more efficient. Even though the Navy had been cut back the industrial sinew needed to expand it rapidly was in existence and getting stronger. There were about 110 sail of the line, most of them in Ordinary or in home squadrons. Traditionally a reinforcement of the Channel Squadron was the first step in an emergency, but in 1793 there was also an urgent need to create a Mediterranean Squadron. The south of France was still staunchly monarchist, and as Toulon was in anti-Revolutionary hands there was a chance to occupy the port, neutralise the French Fleet and deal a body-blow to the Revolution.

Above left: HMS *Britannia*, a 1st Rate 120-gun ship.

Above right: A typically bloody boarding scene showing the hazards of splinters and falling spars.

Left: Sir Edward Pellew's brilliant destruction of the *Droits de l'Homme* in 1797, which also resulted in the loss of HMS *Indefatigable*.

The man chosen to lead the expedition was Lord Hood, who hoisted his flag in the 100-gun 1st Rate *Victory*, and among the 20 ships of the line under his command was the 64-gun *Agamemnon*, under the command of Captain Horatio Nelson. The brightest star in the galaxy of talent which the war was to create, Nelson was 34 years old and had entered the Royal Navy in 1770. Unlike Admiral Hood, Nelson came from a comparatively modest background, being the son of a Norfolk clergyman, and had only obtained a place as a midshipman through the influence of his uncle, Captain Maurice Suckling. This was a common method of entry for youngsters, as each captain had the right to appoint two 'servants' – a fiction which has caused some confusion to a later generation about the social origins of naval officers.

Hood's biggest problem was the manning of his squadron, for the harshness of life afloat was not mitigated by any generosity on the part of the Admiralty. The pay-scale and conditions of service for seamen had not been changed since the days of Charles II, and the men preferred to serve in merchantmen, for the voyages were generally of shorter duration. To provide the Fleet with the men it needed the Navy had a legal right to 'impress' seamen into the King's Service, and 'Press Gangs' were sent ashore to search the taverns and brothels of Portsmouth, Chatham and Plymouth. In theory impressment was intended to take only trained seamen but inevitably a crop of landsmen, newly-wed bridegrooms, imbeciles and pickpockets were scooped up, and the brutality of the press gang had long since passed into folklore. Gangs of seamen under the command of an experienced officer returned with a bedraggled collection of prisoners minus their belts and braces to prevent them from running away. A returning merchant seaman was liable to be impressed almost in sight of his home port, should a man o' war happen to be short of hands.

The Toulon force finally got to sea in May 1793, and after escorting an incoming convoy, set sail for Cadiz. One of the oddities of this war was that it threw Spain and England together for the first time in their history, and a joint Anglo-Spanish squadron was formed off Toulon, when Hood was joined by the Spanish Admiral de Langara. The joint force instituted a blockade of Marseilles and Toulon, waiting for a sign from the anti-Jacobin forces. On 23rd August in response to a request from the citizens of Toulon, the Allies moved in, occupying the dockyard and harbour, and taking possession of the 20 French ships there.

The occupation of France's major naval base was a remarkable achievement, but little could be done to exploit it. For one thing Hood had been given only two regiments, and these were insufficient to man the defences of the town, even with the help of sailors and marines from the fleet. There was also a problem of divided loyalties; although the Spanish contingent had no affection for the Jacobins, and were as eager as the English to deal a mortal blow to the Revolution, they knew that if the French Fleet came under Royal Navy control it would, sooner or later, be used against Spain. Equally the Toulon-

Above: Sir William Sidney Smith, who had something of Nelson's originality of mind but not his ability to work with other officers.

Below: The flagship *Queen Charlotte* (100 guns) leading a review in Spithead in 1790.

assembled to punish Toulon and to win it back from the enemy. Among his officers was a young Corsican artilleryman, Napoleon Buonaparte – future historians would enjoy the irony of the future Emperor of France facing Nelson, the man who would frustrate his grand design, but neither man was aware of the other's existence. It was Buonaparte who made his mark, however, for he directed the artillery with conspicuous succcess, enabling a key position to be taken by assault on 16th December. The following day Hood held a council of war, which convinced him that Toulon was no longer capable of being defended. The decision was made to evacuate the defenders and to burn or tow away the French warships. Captain Sir Sidney Smith was given this task with a small party of Spanish, and as the doomed city came under a heavy bombardment and infantry assault he set about burning what he could. Amid scenes resembling Dante's Inferno Smith achieved considerable success: nine French ships of the line burned or sunk and four towed away, including the giant 120-gun *Commerce de Marseille*. By dawn on 19th December the ships of the fleet could take stock. They had rescued 8000 troops and nearly 15,000 refugees, but the rest of the populace had been abandoned to the fury of the Jacobins. In Lamartine's words, 'The guillotine entered Toulon with the artillery, and blood flowed. . . .' By the time the Deputies of the Convention had slaked their bloodlust 6000 people had been guillotined.

The fall of Toulon left the British dangerously exposed. Without Minorca it was difficult to maintain a blockade of Toulon and Marseilles; in theory Spain was still an ally, throughout she remained lukewarm, and the Italian states were now clamouring for aid in resisting Jacobin subversion, and could not be relied upon to help.

nais, however devout their destestation of Jacobinism, were none too happy about their ancestral foe being admitted to the arsenal and dockyard. But above all, Hood and his officers reckoned without the energy of the Revolution. A large army under General Carteau had already been

Hood's subsequent operations in Corsica were marred by squabbles with his army commanders. The lessons of the Seven Years' War were forgotten, and Hood was denied the benefit of the harmony and understanding between the two services which is vital to combined operations. It had started at Toulon, when Major General David Dundas had been against the admiral's attempt to hold Toulon for as long as possible. In fact the whole enterprise might have been successful if Sir Robert Boyd, the senile Governor of Gibraltar, had been willing to allow some of his garrison to be used to reinforce the troops at Toulon. When Hood decided on his attempt to seize Corsica (with a view to providing his fleet with a secure base well inside the Mediterranean) the soldiers were most enthusiastic about the prospect of collaboration with the Corsican guerrillas, but then lapsed into extreme pessimism. A contemporary described Hood as 'extremely sanguine' whereas Dundas had the opposite qualities of 'caution and backwardness', so it is hardly surprising that there was discord, but the interservice rivalry was exacerbated by the arrival of Lieutenant Colonel John Moore. His touchiness was combined with a mercurial temperament, and he continued

Above: The young Nelson, whose contemporaries quickly recognised his abilities.

Below: A merchantman and a yacht off Dover, typical of the coastal commerce vital to Britain's survival.

Above: An early portrait of Richard Howe, victor at the Glorious First of June.

Below: Sir William Cornwallis, 'Billy Blue', also as a young man.

It was during these operations that Nelson lost the sight of his right eye. He had been on land with guns and men from the *Agamemnon* during the siege of Calvi, and on 12th July 1794 a round shot had pitched short in front of him, throwing sand into the eye. Only later did he realise that it was a permanent injury to the pupil. Contrary to popular myth the eyeball did not have to be removed, and when in later life the sight of his left eye began to deteriorate he was forced to wear an eye-shade over it – not a black eyepatch.

Back home, the Channel Squadron under Lord Howe was more concerned with bringing the Brest Fleet to action. Like Hood, Howe had severe manning problems and did not get to sea until July 1793. The traditional blockade of the French coast was immediately enforced, but the French gave Howe no chance until the following spring. The Revolution was in a parlous state, with widespread shortages of food, and a vital grain convoy was expected from the West Indies. Modern scholars question the contemporary belief that the grain convoy was so vital that its interception could have brought about the fall of the Convention and (presumably) the collapse of France's armies, but the fact remains that Admiral Villaret Joyeuse was ordered to save it at all costs, and he took the Brest Squadron to sea on 16th May 1794.

Howe had been cruising off Ushant, and on his return he was dismayed to find that Brest was empty, the French fleet having left three days earlier. On 28th May one of

his 74s, HMS *Audacious*, unwisely took on the 110-gun three-decker *Revolutionnaire*, and after a terrible battering for two hours she had to break off and make for Plymouth. But other ships had inflicted damage on the French 1st Rate, and she only escaped when darkness fell. The two fleets were in contact the following day but when fog came down all activity came to an end. The fog continued until 1st June, when Howe sighted his opponent only six miles to leeward.

The British fleet was in line abreast, and the action started at about 9 am. The flagship *Queen Charlotte* made a determined attempt to break the French line, passing under the stern of Villaret-Joyeuse's flagship, the 120-gun *Montagne*. The British 1st Rate fired a broadside as she passed and was preparing to luff up when a shot brought down her fore topmast; she was forced to remain on the *Montagne*'s quarter, but played such a fierce fire on her opponent that she was forced to bear away out of the line. As soon as he saw the French line losing its cohesion Howe hoisted the 'Chase' signal.

The rest of the Channel Squadron was also inflicting heavy damage on the French. The *Leviathan* battered *l'Amerique* to a hulk, and the Frenchman shortly afterwards struck her colours to the 1st Rate *Royal Sovereign*. Similarly the *Marlborough* reduced the *Impetueux* to a sinking condition, but the fiercest fight of all took place between the *Brunswick* and the *Vengeur*. For nearly three hours the two ships battered each other, and when they drifted apart the *Brunswick* had lost 45 killed and 113 wounded; before the

quired to get a big fleet to sea take a generation or more to acquire, and they cannot be neglected for any length of time. The sea is such a demanding element that the mere act of operating at sea helps to weed out incompetents, whereas a peacetime army tends to accumulate people who are unsuited to wartime conditions. Certainly in the Revolutionary War the Royal Navy returned to peak efficiency far faster than the British Army, in spite of also being maladministered.

Once again the French sugar islands in the West Indies became a strategic objective, but this time a descent on Martinique was unsuccessful as too few ships and men were sent. A second attempt early in February 1794 had a happier outcome, largely because Vice-Admiral Sir John Jervis and General Sir Charles Grey showed an exemplary grasp of inter-service cooperation. Martinique's governor, General Rochambeau, surrendered

on 27th March, and by July St Lucia and Guadeloupe were in British hands as well.

In this war the Royal Navy brought all its experience of previous wars with France together to make its Brest blockade effective. In May 1795 Vice-Admiral William Cornwallis took a squadron of five sail of the line from Spithead to take up his position off Ushant, and from then on a remorseless grip fastened on the main French fleet. 'Billy Blue' Cornwallis achieved a remarkable personal dominance, for his blockading frigates and sloops had to keep on station in all weathers, running the risk of being attacked by a French squadron. Their task was above all to report on any movement of the French, 'to look into Brest to see if the French had their yards crossed', as contemporary reports so often phrased it. Crossed yards indicated that the Brest Squadron was getting ready to put to sea, but for the most part the great ships lay

Above: The Battle of Cape St Vincent in 1797 eliminated the risk of the Spanish Navy joining the French Toulon Fleet.

Right: A wood panel commemorating the Royal Navy's greatest admirals and their victories.

Vengeur sank 400 of her crew were rescued, including the gallant Captain Renaudin. During the engagement the *Achille* had tried to come to the rescue of the *Vengeur*, but a broadside from the *Brunswick* dismasted her. She too struck her colours.

The Glorious First of June, so called because it was too far out into the Atlantic to be named after a convenient point on the map, was something of a disappointment to the Royal Navy. When it was learned afterwards that the great convoy of American grain had given the Revolution a new lease of life there was considerable criticism of 'Black Dick' Howe. But he had given the nation a victory at a moment when it was sorely needed. The execution of King Louis and Marie Antoinette and the Reign of Terror caused more than a shiver of apprehension in England, while the failure of the remaining European nations to overthrow the ill-disciplined French armies promised a long and exhausting war. Even without the convoy the captures were impressive enough: the 80-gun ships *Sanspareil* and *Juste*, the 74s *Amerique*, *Impetueux*, *Achille* and *Northumberland*. It also served as a dire warning to the French Navy that in sea warfare, unlike land warfare, patriotism and revolutionary fervour are not sufficient. The basic skills re-

ENGLAND EXPECTS *Every MAN to do his DUTY.*

Above: Howe's flagship HMS *Queen Charlotte* heavily engaged at the Glorious First of June.

under the cover of the guns of the Arsenal. Year in, year out, the British ships kept their watch, suffering scurvy and seasickness. More important was the toll on ships, for a wooden man o' war had never been intended to take a continuous battering from the sea. The ancient term for the Reserve Fleet, 'lying in Ordinary', itself indicates that ships were intended to

spend more time laid up in dockyard than at sea. Fortunately the Royal Dockyards proved as efficient as they had in the American War, and a ceaseless trickle of refitted ships, with new masts, repaired guns and newly coppered bottoms returned to service.

Had Nelson not achieved the fame which he did later Hood's successor as commander of the Mediterranean Fleet might today be regarded as the Royal Navy's greatest sailor. Sir John Jervis had been promoted Admiral of the Blue in

June 1795 and was 60 years old when appointed to the most crucial command. With no rich connections, the life of the young Jervis had been harsh – his father had given him £20 at the age of 14, to set him up in life. Although gifted with considerable humour his experience of poverty left him with a stern, puritanical devotion to duty, and he well earned his reputation as a slave-driver and strict disciplinarian. When asked why he disapproved of the barbarous punishment of 'flogging around the Fleet', whereby the

Above: Howe (left) and his staff on the quarterdeck of the *Queen Charlotte* as the dying Captain Neville of the Queen's Regiment is carried below.

prisoner was taken to each ship in the fleet in turn and severly flogged at each stop, 'Jarvie' is reputed to have said that it was far too uneconomical a method of execution. Even more telling was another dictum, 'Responsibility is the test of a man's courage.'

Jervis reached Gibraltar at the end of November 1795, to find that his iron resolution was sorely needed. The ships of the Mediterranean Fleet were in poor condition after so long at sea – the capture of Elba and Corsica was no compensation for the lack of the excellent British-built dockyard at Port Mahon in Minorca. The Jacobin cause seemed close to triumph, and even in Britain there were prominent Whigs who favoured an understanding with Revolutionary France. But Jervis took no account of all these factors when he took command on 29th November. That day, after his frigate HMS *Lively* had taken up her position at the head of the fleet, lying at anchor in Gibraltar harbour, he ordered the fleet to weigh anchor. By nightfall a close blockade of Toulon had been started, and it was to continue without respite for eight months.

The smack of firm authority put new heart into the Royal Navy, and at the same time dislocated French plans for a seizure of the Papal States' fleet at Civitavecchia. His discipline was tempered with concern for the welfare of his men. Fresh meat and vegetables were obtained regularly, and every fortnight storeships took water and

Left: HMS *Brunswick* engaging the *Vengeur du Peuple* and the *Achille.* In spite of heavy odds she survived, sinking one and dismasting the other.

Above: Admiral Sir George Cockburn presiding over the burning of the White House in 1814.

victuals to the blockaders lying off Toulon. For the first time a commander in chief took the step of insisting on regular collection and delivery of mail, and he even saw to such luxuries as a supply of tobacco. Jervis also introduced the Colours ceremony, still standard in the Royal Navy. No-one who witnesses 'Sunset' on the quarterdeck can fail to be stirred by the salute to the Colours as they are lowered. Not for nothing was a later French historian to say that the day on which Admiral Jervis hoisted his flag aboard HMS *Victory* was the day on which the Royal Navy began its career of conquest.

On land the situation was nothing like so reassuring. One by one the allies of 1793 were overwhelmed or simply reverted to older alignments. Holland was attacked in 1795, Spain returned to the French fold in August 1796, and at about the same time

Genoa and Leghorn were 'persuaded' to close their ports to British shipping. The fervour of the Convention had given way to the corrupt ineptitude of the Directory, but by way of compensation the young General Buonaparte had started to win a series of victories in northern Italy.

There was need of a man of Jervis' calibre, for Britain now stood alone. The Directory, propped up by Napoleon Buonaparte's victories, was confident that it could launch an invasion of England, and it had good reason for optimism. The large Dutch fleet was available, as was the French fleet at Brest, while the Mediterranean boasted the Spanish and a string of satellite countries. If all these dis-

parate elements could be combined and a Franco-Spanish squadron concentrated at Brest, surely the haughty islanders could at last be brought to heel. As Napoleon himself put it, in a letter to the Directory, 'If the Republic were once master of the Mediterranean the campaign would speedily terminate, but the presence of the British squadron impedes this.'

Clearly the counter to this threat was to prevent the junction of the French and Spanish fleets, and so important was this objective that the British Government was even prepared to abandon the Mediter-ranean. Such a step was a bitter blow but there was no choice, and Corsica and Elba were evacuated and plans were drafted to take the fleet to Lisbon, for Gibraltar offered poor protection from the winter gales. Yet even out of this disaster captains like Nelson were able to wring an advantage. In December 1796, while fly-ing his pennant as a Commodore in the frigate *Minerve*, he managed to capture a Spanish frigate and chase off a second; much to his chagrin he was forced to abandon his prize, *La Sabina*, when two enemy ships of the line appeared.

In the light of all that has been said, the decision to abandon the Mediterranean was a measure of how desperately over-stretched the Royal Navy had become. But the facts were overwhelming: Jervis had only 14 sail of the line against 30 or more,

Left: Nelson receives the sword of a dying Spanish captain at the Battle of Cape St Vincent.

Below: Admiral Jervis deployed an Inshore Squadron to keep a close watch on Cadiz in 1797.

and there was such a shortage of supplies that rations were cut by two-thirds. Although fire-eaters like Nelson swore that the withdrawal was unnecessary it had to be done, and even so skilled a leader as Jervis was forced to use a subterfuge to draw the French away towards Cagliari in order to leave the way for his weary ships and exhausted, half-starved sailors to get to Gibraltar safely. To make matters worse Irish nationalists under Wolfe Tone were ready to raise the standard of revolt in Ireland; fortunately an attempt to get 18,000 French troops across to Ireland miscarried, but there remained the threat of a large French in-vasion fleet in the Channel Ports. As Jervis put it, 'A victory is very essential to England at this moment.'

That moment came on 13th February 1797 when lookouts aboard HMS *Blenheim* sighted strange sails to the south west. Two nights earlier Nelson in the frigate *Minerve* had actually sailed *through* the Spanish Fleet without being recognised, and now Jervis knew that the battle which he and his men craved so desperately was about to begin. The signal was made to prepare for battle late in the afternoon, and when night fell Jervis ordered his ships to keep in close order so as to be ready for action at first light. He himself retired to his cabin, not to sleep but to arrange his papers and to make his will. Having done this he wrote some letters until just before daybreak, when he returned to the quarterdeck to await events.

The Battle of Cape St Vincent came about because the Spanish Fleet was escorting a valuable convoy of five mercury ships from Malaga to Cadiz. Mercury was vital in the refining of silver from South America, the staple of the Spanish economy, and to safeguard the mercury ships Admiral Don Jose de Cordoba had 27 sail of the line. He sailed from Cartagena on 1st February, escorting an ordinary convoy, and called at Malaga to collect the mercury ships. Having delivered his precious charges to Cadiz his orders were then to proceed to Brest, where his squadron would join the French for the projected invasion of Ireland and England in turn. Unfortunately he was desperately short of trained seamen, and had to put to sea with as few as 60-80 per ship. The rest were pressed landsmen or soldiers, who would be a handicap no matter how bravely they fought. Even so, the odds were impressive, 27 sail of the line including the largest wooden man o'

Above: The victory won by Jervis at Cape St Vincent was a notable achievement by the Royal Navy at a time of exceptional stress.

war ever built, the 136-gun *Santissima Trinidad*, against 15 British three- and two-deckers.

Once again the British determination to break the enemy line gave them the initiative, and the Spanish had little option but to conform to the moves of the two columns bearing down on them from the north. As HMS *Culloden* approached the Spanish line her 1st Lieutenant remarked to Captain Troubridge that there was insufficient room to pass between two towering 1st Rates. Troubridge merely replied that the weakest must fend off, and waited until the moment of collision before giving the order to fire. At little more than six yards' distance the rippling double-shotted broadside tore into the Spanish ship, sending up a huge cloud of splinters and wood-dust. Her opponent swung right around under the shock, revealing her opposite broadside, but as she had not expected to be engaged on that side the guns were not manned, and the *Culloden* passed down the line virtually unscathed. Troubridge was expecting orders to tack, and no sooner had the flags run up the *Victory*'s halyards than his ship acknowledged the signal and began to turn. On seeing this example of discipline Jervis lost his usual reserve and shouted to his Master, 'Look at Troubridge there. He tacks his ship into battle as if the eyes of England were upon him – and would to God they were.'

Meanwhile the rest of the Fleet was coming into action. Lucky hits on the foremast of HMS *Colossus* caused her to lose way and swerve across the bows of the *Irresistible* and *Victory* coming up astern. In trying to avoid her the *Victory* had to

Left: Lord Keith commanded in the North Sea from 1803 to 1807 and conducted operations against the French invasion forces.

Right: Duncan's opponent at Camperdown, the Dutch Vice Admiral de Winter.

Far right: John Cranford, a gallant sailor who nailed the flagship *Venerable*'s colours to the mast after the halyards were shot away.

slow almost to a halt, opening a gap in the line, and Vice-Admiral Juan Joaquin Moreno in the 112-gun *Principe de Asturias* thought that he saw a chance of breaking the British line. He reckoned without the *Victory*, whose captain waited imperturbably as the giant three-decker bore down on her fast, threatening a collision which could easily be fatal to both ships. At the last moment the Spaniard's nerve broke and she swerved to clear the *Victory*, giving the flagship the chance to pour in one of those terrible double-shotted broadsides. Reeling under the blow the gallant *Principe de Asturias* continued to turn, allowing the *Victory* to rake her stern galleries, killing and wounding yet more men on her crowded decks.

Cordoba was still full of fight, and ordered seven ships at the head of his line to concentrate on the British rear, and catch them between two fires. It would have been a bold stroke, but it was badly executed because of the inexperience of the Spanish crews. There was also Nelson, now flying his broad pennant in the two-deck *Captain*. Realising what was happening he ordered Captain Miller to run towards the massive formation, intending to hold them up until other ships could join him. Jervis saw the *Captain* leave the line, and immediately realised what Nelson was trying to achieve; up went the signal 'Take suitable stations for mutual support' in the hope that the *Captain* could survive long enough.

It was a close-run thing, for even with the help of Captain Collingwood in HMS *Excellent* there were only two 74s against seven Spanish ships. The *Captain* was terribly battered, but eventually the *Culloden* and other ships came up to take some of the strain. Nelson's crippled 74 was run alongside the 80-gun ship *San Nicolas*, allowing the British boarding parties to swarm over her bulwarks and capture her. In the meantime the 112-gun *San Josef* had collided with the *San Nicolas* on the other side, so the *Captain*'s boarding parties made ready to board her as well, but she then surrendered. Throughout the fleet the *San Nicolas* was described as 'Nelson's Patent Bridge for

Left: Table Bay at the Cape of Good Hope, by Hodges.

Right: Camperdown marked the end of Holland as a first-class naval power.

John Cranford, of Sunderland, Durham.
The Sailor who nailed the Flag to the Main Top gallant mast head.
on board the Venerable, Lord Duncan's Ship, after being
once Shot away by the Dutch Admiral de Winter.

Drawn by Mr Orme on board for the Express purpose of Introducing into his
Picture of Lord Duncan's Victory now Engraving by Subscription & which includes Portraits
of the Admirals & Officers who so Gloriously Distinguished themselves on the
ever Memorable 11th of October 1797.

Proposals may be had & Subscriptions Received by Mr Orme.

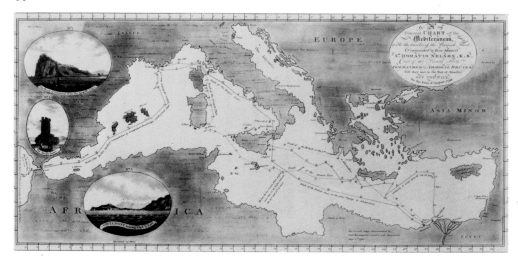

Above: Contemporary map of the Mediterranean showing Nelson's pursuit of the French Toulon Fleet, which ended in the Battle of the Nile.

Boarding Three-Deckers', recognition of this unique incident.

When the weary victors counted their prizes that evening they found that they had taken two three-deckers, the giant *Salvador del Mundo* and *San Josef* and two two-deckers, *San Nicolas* and *San Isidro*. Several others had surrendered, but in the confusion had subsequently rehoisted their colours and rejoined the flagship. Next morning revealed that the Spaniards were still in sight, but although the plucky Cordoba wished to renew the fight his ships were too sorely battered to be able to comply with his orders. As

Jervis had said, it was a victory which England sorely needed, and it heartened the Royal Navy when morale was low.

Charles Dibdin, creator of Tom Bowling, expressed British popular feeling in a verse which caught the imagination:
'Howe made the Frenchmen dance a tune,
An admiral great and glorious:
Witness for that the First of June –
Lord, how he was victorious!
A noble sight as e'er was seen,
And did the country service;
But twenty-seven beat with fifteen
None ever did but Jervis!'
The euphoria inspired by the victory was all the more rudely dispelled, therefore, when news came through that the ships lying at Spithead and the Nore had refused to go to sea.

The Great Mutinies of 1797 immediately raised the spectre of Jacobinism but no evidence of any outside subversion was ever found. The real cause was poor pay, aggravated by rising inflation of the war-time economy and an inequitable system of victualling. The pay had not been changed for more than a century, but above all the rascally pursers were permitted to keep back an eighth of all rations. To prevent desertion the ship's company was not paid until the end of a commission – to this day the Royal Navy calls decommissioning 'paying off' – and in addition they were paid in Admiralty vouchers. These 'tickets' had been a grievance in the Dutch Wars, for they could only be cashed in London. Rather than squander his hard-earned pay on a long and expensive trip to London a sailor was usually tempted to cash his 'ticket' with one of the brokers to be found in the naval ports, but at a substantial discount.

A modern theory to account for the sudden upsurge of unrest is the effect of the Quota Acts passed to combat the chronic shortage of manpower. This legislation required towns within a short distance of the sea to provide a 'quota' of men for the Navy. In theory this would provide a cross-section of able-bodied men but in practice astute parish councils emptied the jails. The effect of this was that the Navy received a sudden influx of petty criminals, mental defectives and other substandard recruits who did nothing for efficiency or morale. Another theory put

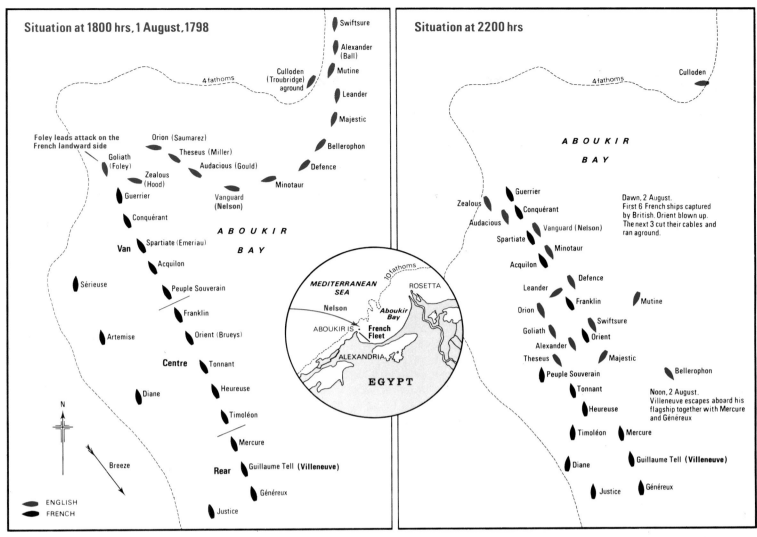

Situation at 1800 hrs, 1 August, 1798

4 fathoms

Swiftsure
Alexander (Ball)
Culloden (Troubridge) aground
Mutine
Leander
Majestic
Bellerophon
Defence
Minotaur

Foley leads attack on the French landward side

Orion (Saumarez)
Theseus (Miller)
Audacious (Gould)
Goliath (Foley)
Zealous (Hood)
Vanguard (Nelson)
Guerrier
Conquérant
Van
Spartiate (Emeriau)
Sérieuse
Acquilon
Peuple Souverain
Franklin
Artemise
Orient (Brueys)
Centre
Tonnant
Diane
Heureuse
Timoléon
Mercure
Rear
Guillaume Tell (Villeneuve)
Généreux
Justice

A B O U K I R   B A Y

N

Breeze

◗ ENGLISH
● FRENCH

Situation at 2200 hrs

4 fathoms

Culloden

A B O U K I R   B A Y

Zealous
Guerrier
Conquérant
Audacious
Vanguard (Nelson)
Spartiate
Minotaur
Acquilon
Defence
Leander
Franklin
Mutine
Orion
Swiftsure
Goliath
Orient
Alexander
Theseus
Majestic
Peuple Souverain
Bellerophon
Tonnant
Heureuse
Timoléon
Mercure
Diane
Guillaume Tell (Villeneuve)
Justice
Généreux

Dawn, 2 August.
First 6 French ships captured by British. Orient blown up. The next 3 cut their cables and ran aground.

Noon, 2 August.
Villeneuve escapes aboard his flagship together with Mercure and Généreux

MEDITERRANEAN SEA
10 fathoms
ROSETTA
Nelson
Aboukir Bay
ABOUKIR IS.
French Fleet
ALEXANDRIA
EGYPT

Left: The blowing up of the French flagship casts a lurid glow over the Battle of the Nile.

forward is that among these 'quota men' was a sprinkling of educated men who had found themselves in prison for debt. These men were able to explain to their illiterate comrades just what their real entitlements were.

In fact the Spithead mutiny was not so much a mutiny as a sitdown strike. All the anonymous petitions and round robins addressed to the Admiralty stressed that the men would sail 'if the French came out', but until then they would accept no orders. What is certain is that the harsh code of discipline was not at issue; in several cases mutineers were flogged by their shipmates for insulting officers. The Nore ships, however, fell under the sway of an unbalanced agitator, Richard Parker, who tried to proclaim a floating republic. To add to his misdemeanours he tried to blockade the Thames to prevent food from reaching London. The Admiralty, having brought the crisis upon itself by ignoring all the warning signs, did the right thing by appointing the popular 'Black Dick' Howe as a negotiator, with full powers to deal with the mutineers. Under his patient guidance the men were persuaded to return to work, but at the Nore Parker's intransigence prevented any

such settlement. Finally individual ships began to desert Parker's cause, as news spread that the Spithead Committees had won all the concessions which had been demanded. As promised by Howe, no reprisals were exacted from the Spithead ships, but Richard Parker ended his short life by being hanged at the yardarm.

If proof were needed that the Royal Navy had recovered its equilibrium, the Battle of Camperdown on 11th October 1797 provided it. Admiral Adam Duncan had been as badly affected by the mutinies as anyone, and at one stage had been reduced to a single ship. In this remarkable action the British showed the same eagerness to be at their enemies as they had in the Dutch Wars, and Camperdown can hardly be rated as a great tactical battle. What it is famous for, however, is the great accuracy and rapidity of the gunnery. The defeated Dutch Admiral de Winter said afterwards that Duncan's ships had fired three times as fast as the Dutch. It was also the bloodiest battle of the war; the figure of 203 killed and 620 wounded on the English side, with 540 Dutch killed and 620 wounded gives some idea of the ferocity of the fighting. More important was the fact that this single action knocked the Dutch out of the contest and robbed the French of their most useful asset. Indeed, modern Dutch his-

Above: Nelson destroying revolutionary crocodiles, Gillray's satirical view of the Battle of the Nile.

torians regard Camperdown (or Kamperduin) as the end of Dutch aspirations to first-class naval power.

These hard blows did nothing to deflect the French from their grand design of supremacy in the Mediterranean. With no British squadron stationed there throughout 1797 it was tempting to think of invading Egypt and even advancing on India. By February 1798 Buonaparte was collecting ships and men for an attack on Egypt, and although the preparations were carried out in secrecy the British got wind of them and appointed the newly promoted Rear-Admiral Sir Horatio Nelson to command a new Mediterranean Squadron. Nelson had a brief to find out exactly what the French Toulon Fleet was up to, and from May to July he fretfully sought out the enemy without result. By a series of mischances he failed to stop the French from taking Malta and then arrived at Alexandria ahead of the French expeditionary force. Not until 1st August did Nelson find the French, a large fleet under Admiral Brueys anchored in Aboukir Bay, not far from Alexandria. He had thirteen 74-gun ships, including his own flagship HMS *Vanguard*, and the 50-gun ship *Leander*, while Brueys could muster the giant 120-gun *l'Orient*, three 80s, nine 74s and four frigates.

The line of French ships curved towards the shore, apparently protected by shoals, and when it was pointed out to Nelson that there was a gap between the 74 *Guerriere* and a small island at the northern end of the bay he decided that it might be possible to work his ships through, to fight *inside* the French line. If Brueys thought that he could not be attacked that night he was badly mistaken, for at 4 pm Nelson ordered his ships to

move in. When he judged that sufficient ships were inside he took the *Vanguard* on the outside, and anchored opposite the *Spartiate*. The other ships also anchored to prevent their sterns swinging with the current, and they were now in a unique position of double envelopment. The unfortunate French line was now demolished piecemeal, outnumbered at one end of the line but unable to get the remainder of the line into action to offset the concentration. By 9 pm the *Guerriere*, *Conquérant* and *Spartiate* had surrendered. The giant *l'Orient* had punished the *Bellerophon* but had then been damaged severely by the combined efforts of the *Alexander* and *Swiftsure*. Brueys was mortally wounded when a round shot struck him, and at about 9 pm the flagship caught fire (she was rumoured to have some sort of 'infernal machine' or mine on board). An hour later she blew up with a tremendous explosion, an event so frightening that for some minutes there was no firing.

At dawn a grim sight was revealed. Out of the entire French fleet only the *Guillaume Tell* and the *Généreux*, and the frigates *Diane* and *Justice* were able to make their escape. The others were all dismasted or aground. It was the most decisive victory the Royal Navy had achieved to date – the sort of victory that Nelson yearned after, total and conclusive. It scotched Napoleon's plans for an attack on the East, and in the short term it stirred up resistance in Europe to French hegemony. It also weakened French sea power in the Mediterranean to a fatal extent, and elevated Nelson to a pinnacle of fame which exceeded even that of Jervis (now Earl St Vincent). He was made Baron of the Nile, Parliament voted him a pension of £2000 a year, and the East India Company made him an outright gift of £10,000.

Critics of the little admiral called him

vain and overkeen to collect honours, but there was something essentially modest about Nelson. In an intensively competitive service he made only two professional enemies, and the rest of the service worshipped him. At Cape St Vincent he had displayed great tactical sense, but no greater than his superior, Jervis. At the Nile he showed that he was a brilliant tactician, capable of sizing up a situation quickly. If he had fought only those two actions his reputation would still outrank any other British officer, but within seven years he was to give his country an even greater victory.

Right: Nelson, wearing a bandage after sustaining a head wound, exhorting his men at the Nile.

Below: The British under Sir Ralph Abercromby land in Egypt in 1801 to complete Nelson's victory by routing the French Army at the Battle of the Pyramids.

The badly battered *Victory* is towed to Gibraltar after the Battle of Trafalgar.

Sea Power vs Land Power

Above left: Admiral Sir Hyde Parker, Nelson's superior at Copenhagen.

Above right: The Danish line of hulks and floating batteries, which had to be breached before Nelson's ships could get at the Danish Fleet.

As the 18th century drew to its close the war between Great Britain and France had reached something approaching a stalemate. Both contestants were weary and anxious to see an end to hostilities, but both had achieved important gains at great cost which could not be sacrificed lightly.

The new ruler of France, Napoleon Buonaparte, was not yet sufficiently secure, and so he called for peace negotiations. The Peace of Amiens lasted from 1802 to 1803, and gave both antagonists a much-needed respite, but it was doomed for the simple reason that Napoleon, now Emperor of France, had fresh plans for the conquest of Europe. He had still not comprehended fully the reasons underlying the British successes, the fact that an accident of geography had placed the British Isles across the exits from the Baltic and the Channel, that the prevailing winds blow in from the Atlantic, and that there was a lack of good harbours on the French coast. Nor did the 'Corsican ogre' realise that British shipyards now had access to timber from Canada and America, just at the time when the supplies of English oak were beginning to be exhausted.

Napoleon's solution to sea power was to revive the concept of the Armed Neutrality which had caused Britain so much worry in the American War 20 years earlier. A first attempt in 1801 had been aborted by Nelson's brilliant action at Copenhagen, when his ships silenced the Danish coastal batteries and threaded their way through the shoals to destroy the Danish Fleet. It was a short and brutal action but it had the desired effect: the junior member of a nascent Armed Neutrality was knocked out, and what was even more beneficial, the warships were no longer available to serve French interests. Further action was contemplated against Russia but after the assassination of the mad Tsar Paul Russia suddenly decided to leave the Armed Neutrality, and the French were back where they had started.

The next attempt to outflank sea power was much more elaborate. The Army of England was to be assembled to invade Britain, and to enable it to cross the Channel in a huge flotilla of flat-bottomed boats the Royal Navy must be decoyed away. The idea was hardly new but there was one element of subtlety. This time small detachments would slip out of French ports (they would have a much better chance of slipping through the blockade than a large squadron), head for a secret rendezvous, and then swoop back while the Royal Navy was dispersed

around the world searching for them. The difficult part would still be the Channel crossing: estimates of the time varied from six hours to six weeks, to get as many as 150,000 men, as well as horses, artillery and supply wagons across. Leaving aside the most pessimistic and the ludicrously over-optimistic forecasts, French Army experts said that they needed at least 14 days to get this force to its destination, and that was the first of the 'ifs' which appeared. Like the previous English invasion scheme in 1759 there were altogether too many of these 'ifs'. Napoleon's master plan failed to take account of the vagaries of wind and weather, and above all, failed to allow for any refusal by the British to behave as he had predicted. In fact the British response was exactly as it had been in 1588 and subsequently: the Admiralty ordered its squadrons to fall back on the Channel, rather than allow them to be dispersed, chasing will o' the wisps. What no land strategists could comprehend was the simple fact that wind and tide can change. For example, Napoleon's orders to Villeneuve to attack Cornwallis from the west while Ganteaume and the Brest Fleet attacked in the rear were bound to fail, simply because the wind needed to bring Villeneuve into action would tend to keep Ganteaume in harbour.

Nelson's task as Commander-in-Chief of the Mediterranean Fleet was to watch

and bring to action the French Mediterranean Fleet under Villeneuve. On 17th January 1805, when he learned that the Toulon Fleet had left harbour, he had no idea that the Emperor's Grand Design was being put in motion. Nobody but the French knew that the secret rendezvous was Martinique, and Nelson assumed that Villeneuve's most likely objectives were Naples, Sicily or Egypt. When a rapid search revealed no trace of the French he assumed that Villeneuve had returned to Toulon. On this occasion he was right, for the French, after being cooped up in harbour for so long, were inclined to be deterred easily by very bad weather. A second wild goose chase seemed to be on the cards when Villeneuve got clear on 30th March, but this time Nelson beat back through the Mediterranean and learned that the French had passed through the Straits of Gibraltar.

Historians have argued ever since over Nelson's subsequent actions, for as soon as he knew that the French were heading for the West Indies he set sail in pursuit all the way across the Atlantic. The French duly arrived at Martinique, but paused only to deal with the British blockade of the sugar islands before heading back to Europe. This time Villeneuve did not re-

Below: Pocock's view of the Battle of Copenhagen, with Nelson's ships replying to the Danish fire.

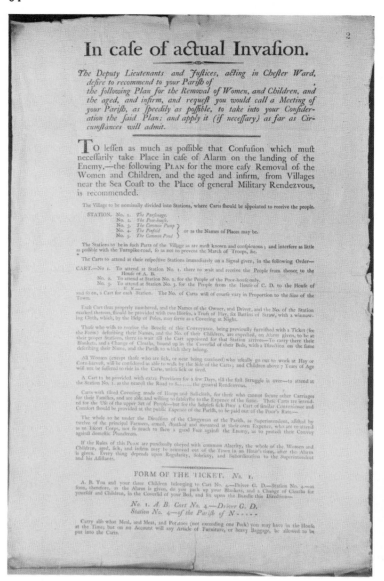

Above: Broadsheet of instructions for the removal of civilians if the French should invade.

turn to Toulon; he was heading for Ferrol, but after a brief action with Sir Robert Calder he was forced to take refuge in Vigo. Nelson could only follow him back, growing more impatient as each day passed, but he did despatch a fast brig, the *Curieux*, with a message to the Admiralty advising that Villeneuve was almost certainly heading for north-west Spain.

The more ardent admirers of Nelson claim that their hero had identified Napoleon's secret rendezvous and by his superior deductive powers had frustrated Napoleon's plan, while his critics claim that he had been panicked into a wild goose chase which had left the English Channel dangerously exposed. The truth seems to lie somewhere between these extremes; Nelson was merely carrying out his orders to safeguard the Mediterranean first, and then to destroy Villeneuve as his second objective. Even though there was an element of comedy in Nelson's fast chase backwards and forwards across the Atlantic he achieved several absolutely vital objectives. First, he discovered that Martinique was the secret rendezvous; second, he saved the West Indies from attack; third, he frightened Villeneuve into returning to Europe *before* the other detachments could reach Martinique; fourth and most important of all, he was able to get the news of Villeneuve's homeward course to the Admiralty before the French arrived.

At this critical point in its history the Royal Navy was lucky in having not only its most imaginative fighting admiral but also its greatest administrator since Pepys. Lord Barham, formerly Charles Middleton, was at 79 well past the age at which First Lords of the Admiralty were supposed to reach their prime, but he matched Nelson's energy in reacting to

Left: Another view of Copenhagen showing Nelson's ships approaching the line of floating batteries and hulks.

Left: A smart boat's crew pulls out to the flagship *Victory*.

Villeneuve to effect a junction with Ganteaume, as if nothing had changed. On 13th August, under repeated exhortations from Paris, Villeneuve got to sea from Ferrol, for the new blockading squadron was not yet in position. For a day the French ships enjoyed their freedom, but knowing full well that the sight of a solitary sail could mean their destruction. Then the wind changed and Villeneuve altered course for Cadiz, where a small Spanish squadron was being watched by Admiral Collingwood. With what has been described as 'complete nonchalance' Collingwood sailed his ships in a circle, making quite certain that the quarry entered the trap, for bringing up the rear were the ships which had been about to blockade Ferrol. Now the Royal Navy knew where its principal adversaries were, and it was happy to have them all in one harbour. It was the end of any pretence at invasion, but the chief culprit could only inveigh against his subordinate Villeneuve, saying 'The wretch had only to obey orders, and victory was won. The failure is his, not mine.'

Barham's master plan was now complete, and it remained only to put the finishing touch by appointing Nelson to command the fleet off Cadiz. It is said that the old man offered Nelson the pick of officers for his new command, but Nelson refused, saying that men of the Royal Navy were of such quality that any of them would be good enough for the task. 'We are,' he said, 'a band of brothers', a phrase which summed up the remarkable fighting machine which had been created for this supreme moment. Nelson had the gift of taking his juniors into his confidence, and of communicating his intentions. This enabled him to keep his plans totally flexible for the coming battle – nothing was committed to paper for the simple reason that there was nothing to commit. Nelson intended to fight the ultimate in battles of opportunity, using the seaman-

events. Early one morning he was awakened to hear the news brought by HMS *Curieux*, and he issued a series of orders which led directly to the Battle of Trafalgar and the total ruin of Napoleon's plans. What Barham was planning was a bold offensive riposte to the French moves, for he actually *relaxed* the blockade in order to improve the Fleet's chances of catching the French at sea – knowing that to be the only way to beat them decisively.

Under Barham's instructions the blockading squadron off Rochefort was to reinforce Sir Robert Calder off Ferrol, and Cornwallis was to lift the blockade of Brest. That remarkable man had already started to do so *before* receiving orders, proof that Barham's plans conformed to a basic British perception of what was required. What the British feared more than any move northwards to the Channel was a move back into the Mediterranean, and to prevent that Barham now divided the Fleet, stationing a large force off Ferrol and using the remaining ships to watch Ganteaume in Brest. All the while

Napoleon sat brooding over the catastrophe which had overtaken his invasion plans. Like another dictator a century later he had made too many public utterances to be able to withdraw from the project but there is not a shadow of doubt that by July 1805 he had privately abandoned all hope of invading England, and had already ordered the Army of England to disperse. And yet, to avoid the humiliation of such an admission, he still ordered the luckless

Right: Royal Navy ships in action off Finisterre in 1804.

Above: Nelson was a remarkable blend of vanity, compassion, daring and competence.

Above right: Trafalgar was Nelson's 'crowning mercy' for it destroyed Napoleon's dream of invading England.

Below: Admiral Nelson was hit by a musket ball fired by a sharpshooter in the maintop of the *Redoutable*.

ship and gunnery skills of his ships rather than drill his captains in a carefully rehearsed set-piece battle. One can only wonder what an early 18th century captain would have made of it all, for Nelson had managed to discard the Fighting Instructions while retaining their intentions.

There is no space in this short history to recount the Battle of Trafalgar in detail, but its broad outlines are very well known. It came about when Villeneuve was finally goaded into putting to sea with 18 French and 15 Spanish ships, bound for the Straits of Gibraltar, in the forlorn hope that he could return to the Mediterranean. Instead he found Nelson implacably barring the way with 27 ships. The British squadron was marshalled in two columns, one led by Collingwood in the three-decker *Royal Sovereign*, the other led by the flagship *Victory*, that same gallant veteran of the American War and the Battle of Cape St Vincent. Contrary to what any theorist would say, Nelson allowed

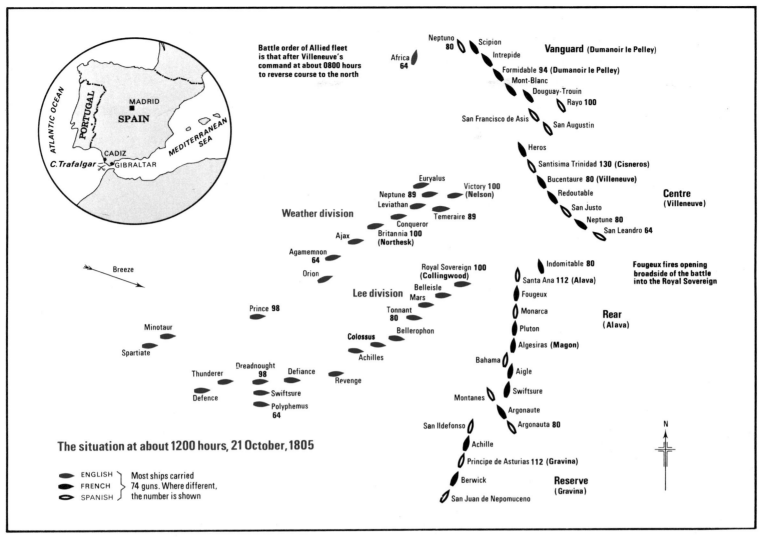

The situation at about 1200 hours, 21 October, 1805

the Franco-Spanish squadron to 'cross his T', exposing his leading ships to the risk of concentrated fire during the approach. But Nelson knew that the French fired high and was banking on their inability to inflict sufficient damage before he was close enough to shatter their formation. There would also be poor cohesion between the French and the Spanish parts of the enemy formation, making it easier for the British plan to succeed. And so it turned out. The British columns were punished heavily as they sailed slowly but inexorably towards the curved line of enemy ships, but the French and Spanish seemed mesmerised by what they saw and failed to take any effective counter-action. Only when the range was down to a few hundred yards did the first British guns fire, and then the rippling broadsides began to inflict awful carnage. It is said that one of HMS *Victory*'s double-shotted broadsides killed 400 men aboard the flagship *Bucentaure* as she passed under her stern.

The *Victory* took tremendous punishment from the *Redoutable*, whose captain, the midget Jean Lucas, was probably the most professional seaman in the French Fleet that day. He and his men put up such a spirited defence that for a time they were convinced that they had silenced the *Victory*'s fire, and Lucas even attempted to board her. It was from his

ship that a sharpshooter fired the shot which killed Nelson on the quarterdeck, but it had no effect on the outcome. All around the French and Spanish ships were being battered into surrender, and the dying Nelson knew that he had gained his beloved country a decisive victory.

Decisive Trafalgar certainly was, for when the firing died away 18 ships had struck their colours, one had blown up and only 11 made their escape to Cadiz. It had been a bloody battle and several of the prizes were so badly damaged that they had to be scuttled; the shortage of unwounded men meant weak prize-crews, and several prizes were subsequently recaptured, so that the final total was only four prizes. Against that, however, could be set a victory which totally transformed the war. It lifted the threat of invasion from British minds, and of course removed other threats such as a landing in Ireland or an attack on overseas colonies. The short-term threat had already been removed but the totality of the victory forced Napoleon finally to realise that he could not fight the Royal Navy. Instead he turned back to his old idea of cutting the British off from European trade. He started to create his 'Continental System', an economic *Festung Europa* to freeze the British out.

The war was to drag on for another ten

years, but in the end it was Napoleon who fell victim to the Continental System rather than Britain. Europe became more and more restive under France's economic and military domination, and Napoleon's legions had to be used to overawe his

Below: The death of Nelson in the cockpit of HMS *Victory*.

so-called allies rather than the British. The exactions of the vast French military machine caused more and more friction, and ultimately Russian discontent with the Continental System forced Napoleon to attempt coercion, a miscalculation which lost him the *Grand Armée*. The British suffered from the loss of their European markets but nothing like as severely as Europe was suffering from the loss of British and overseas markets, for it must be remembered that the Royal Navy blockade prevented hostile ships from trading outside European waters. Another point overlooked by Napoleon was that Britain could develop new markets, and these offset the losses to a large extent.

There were to be no great sea victories for the Royal Navy between 1805 and 1815 although there were countless actions. There was even a short, sharp war with the United States from 1812 until 1814, in which a number of frigates were defeated by the Americans. It was one of those wars which need not have happened – a diplomatic dispute over 'rights of search' and a British habit of removing seamen from American ships on the grounds that they were deserters. The British forces on the North American and West Indies Station were badly over-stretched and could do little to stop the depredations of American privateers but in 1813 the big frigate HMS *Shannon* (50 guns) was sent across to stiffen the defences of the Newfoundland fishing grounds, and in due course she fell in with the USS *Chesapeake*, of approximately the same size and fighting power. The British frigate was commanded by Captain Philip Broke, an exponent of efficient gunnery, and he made short work of the *Chesapeake*. As the war in Europe was now drawing to a close it was also possible to send reinforcements, and when these arrived on the Eastern seaboard the US Navy and the mercantile marine disappeared from the sea. What had seemed a profitable adventure in 1812 became an economic disaster, and it was to be another five years before American overseas trade reached the level of 1812.

It was appropriate that the Royal Navy should play a key role in the last moments of Napoleon's rule. It was a British warship which carried him to Elba, another which received him after his flight from Waterloo, and yet another which took him to his final exile on St Helena. He finally acknowledged their part in his downfall: 'Wherever there is water to float a ship, we are sure to find you in our way.'

The British nation had taken Nelson to its heart before Trafalgar, and his spirit continued to animate the Royal Navy during the ten years' fighting after Trafalgar. It is hard to comprehend the depth of grief throughout the country after the death of the little admiral, for there were no mass communications such as TV and radio, and newspapers were beyond the pocket of the poor. Soon after Nelson had

died in the cockpit of HMS *Victory* the ship's surgeon had taken measures to preserve the body for the long journey home by putting it in a brandy cask. At Gibraltar the brandy was replaced by spirits of wine (wine vinegar), so that there could be time to give the poor, battered *Victory* the repairs she so badly needed.

By the time the ship dropped anchor off St Helens, opposite Portsmouth, on the morning of 4th December 1805 there was an atmosphere of nearly hysterical grief, and there could be no question of allowing the hero to be buried quietly with his parents in Norfolk. The greatest living artists, including John Constable and J M W Turner, were allowed on board to sketch and paint the scene while the damage was still fresh, while literally thousands of ordinary people visited the *Victory*.

Nelson was buried in St Paul's Cathedral, and the whole country was in mourning. Even contemporary furniture was given an ebony inlay as a mark of respect. Even Admiral Villeneuve and Captain Magendie of the *Bucentaure* were paroled to enable them to attend the funeral on 9th January 1806, and no fewer than 160 carriages were in the procession. One of the small number of *Victory*'s seamen who could read and write, recorded that 300 of her seamen marched in the procession, dressed in blue jackets and white trousers with black scarves on their hats and around one arm.

The *Victory* was too valuable to be spared, and was not reduced to Ordinary until the end of 1812, by which time she was in urgent need of a major rebuilding. Even so the Great War against France was running down, and she was recommissioned only as a guardship for Portsmouth, but in view of her prestige as Nelson's flagship she was also to function as the flagship of the Port Admiral, a duty which she took up in January 1824. From that year the custom of holding an annual Trafalgar Dinner on board on 21st October started; on the same day a laurel wreath was hoisted to the masthead and Trafalgar veterans wore laurel wreaths in their hats. As each year went by the old three-decker lay at her moorings, a visible reminder to the nation of what Nelson and the Royal Navy had achieved for them. It is, however, true to say that nobody, and least of all the Admiralty, paid much attention to the preservation of the ship, and it was not until more than a century had passed that the newly founded Society of Nautical Research announced that one of its principal aims would be the preservation of HMS *Victory* as a permanent memorial. That noble aim was interrupted by the First World War, but in 1921 Admiral of the Fleet Lord Milford Haven, the father of Lord Louis Mountbatten, gave a stern warning that the *Victory* was almost beyond repair. A national 'Save the *Victory*' appeal was launched, and such

was the magic of her name and the memory of Nelson and Trafalgar that £180,000 was quickly raised.

On 17th July 1928 King George V officially opened the ship to the public, firmly on dry land in the old No. 2 Dock in Portsmouth Dockyard. She survived the heavy bombing of Portsmouth in 1941, even a near-miss from a 500-lb bomb which burst in the dock. Today she can boast that she has been longer in commission than any other warship, and is visited by over a quarter of a million people each year. She is also an outstanding example of mid-18th-century naval architecture, Slade's

Right: Greenwich Pensioners celebrate the Trafalgar victory on Observatory Hill, by Denning.

Below: The last voyage of the *Victory*, towed to her last resting place in Portsmouth Dockyard in 1922.

greatest masterpiece. Another point of interest is that she was rebuilt after Trafalgar to incorporate Seppings' ideas about protecting the bow from raking fire, and so she also exemplified the improvements introduced in the latter half of the century. Put another way, even if Nelson had not flown his flag at Trafalgar in her, HMS *Victory* would still have been an automatic choice for preservation on account of her unique technical qualities.

While remembering the stirring deeds of the *Victory* and her consorts it is worth reflecting on the astounding achievements of the Royal Navy. Between 1793 and 1814 its ships captured or destroyed 207 enemy ships of the line, twelve 50-gun ships, 339 frigates and 556 sloops and other lesser craft, a grand total of 1114 ships. This figure does not include another 1000 French privateers, nor a large number of American, Danish, Dutch and Spanish privateers.

The Royal Navy at its zenith: Queen Victoria's
Diamond Jubilee Review in 1897.

Pax Britannica

It is often thought that the Royal Navy flourished in the years after Waterloo, but this is far from the case. The naval estimates were cut to the bone, many of the proud two- and three-deckers which had fought so valiantly were laid up in Ordinary, and newer ships were simply never completed. With the disappearance of France from the scene as a serious rival there was no need to maintain a powerful fleet in either the Mediterranean or home waters, and large frigates were left to bear most of the burden of duties. The country was now immensely rich; Britain owned more raw materials and commodities than any other country and had the world's largest merchant fleet.

It could have had disastrous results, with Britain taking over the role of Napoleon as overlord of Europe, but fortunately there were new economic and political philosophies at work. The old theory of mercantilism had given way to Adam Smith's concept of Free Trade, and that doctrine taught that the biggest volume of unrestricted trade would ultimately yield greater profits to all participants. In the realm of political philosophy

it was widely held that material progress and prosperity would cause the disappearance of war, and so there was also a reluctance to sustain large armed forces. Between these two philosophies the Royal Navy had to find a new role, in which it contented itself with building as few large ships as possible and building instead smaller warships which could protect trading interests, survey the world's oceans and put down the piracy which still flourished.

The biggest restriction on the Royal Navy was financial, for the annual Estimates were pared to the bone, in line with the prevailing belief that 'bloated armaments' would soon be a thing of the past. And yet technology was just beginning that series of giant leaps which took mankind into the 20th century, and the men who administered the Royal Navy did their best to keep up to date. There is a widespread belief, put about by quite distinguished writers and scholars, that the Royal Navy devoted all its energy to resisting change – that steamships were an unmitigated nuisance, that iron didn't float, etc., etc. Modern research shows

that some of the absurd comments about steam and iron were not uttered by the admirals concerned, as they had been said in a totally different context in the 1770s. A notorious reactionary comment attributed to Lord Melville about the uselessness of steamships has, on close scrutiny of the Melville papers, turned out not to exist.

To anyone less prejudiced it seems that the early 19th century Navy grappled remarkably well with the vast problems facing it. Far from repudiating steam their Lordships were as avid in adopting it as any commercial shipowner. As early as 1814 the small survey brig *Congo* had been fitted with an experimental engine but it had proved too weak to move her. Seven years later a complete class of paddle steamers was ordered from the Royal Dockyards (the first commercial paddler only started running on the River Thames that year). When the French artilleryman Henri Paixhans proved that hollow spherical shells could be fired from smooth-bore naval guns the Admiralty promptly introduced shell-guns as standard equipment for all classes

of ships, and as soon as a workable screw propeller was available (1838) took it up as an improvement over the paddle-wheel. By May 1840 the Admiralty Board was ready to order its first screw-propelled warship, HMS *Rattler*, and when the famous tug-of-war was held in March 1845 between the *Rattler* and her paddle-driven half-sister HMS *Alecto*, the purpose of the trials was largely to convince the public and Parliament – the Board had already ordered the first of seven screw-driven frigates a year earlier. Finally in September 1846 HMS *Ajax*, the world's first seagoing steam battleship, went to sea. True, she was called a 'screw block-ship' because she was less powerfully armed than contemporary three-deckers, having only 90 guns as against 131, but she was a wooden two-decker whose steam propulsion would enable her to get in and out of action with greater freedom.

The period of peace which came between 1815 and 1914 came to be known as the *Pax Britannica*, for all over the world British warships, mostly small, pursued the task of policing international trade. This also included the suppression

of slavery, for as early as 1807 Great Britain had agreed to outlaw the trade in slaves. Many lives were expended on the heartbreaking tasks of lying off the fever-ridden shores of West Africa, trying to enforce a ban which was flouted as often as possible by ships of other nations. By strenuous diplomatic efforts the British

Above: The 'frigate' *Defence* was one of the fleet of ironclad battleships which followed the *Warrior* and *Black Prince* in the 1860s.

Below: The ironclad floating battery *Terror* ready for launching at Jarrow in April 1856, too late for the Crimean War.

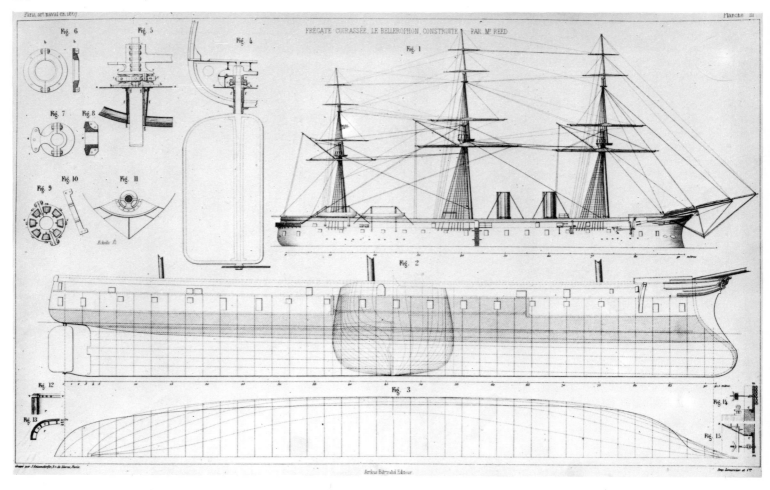

were able to persuade European countries to join in the suppression of slavery, but the United States took much longer to agree.

It was a task which was to last most of the century, and the price paid in lives was heavy. There was a grim little jingle which ran:
'Beware the Bight of Benin,
There's one comes out for forty goes in'
An exaggeration, but a death-rate of one in four was not unknown in the West Coast of Africa Squadron. The death-rate among the slaves was equally terrible, and the sad irony is that the Navy's anti-slavery patrols probably increased the miseries of the slaves; often they were thrown overboard as soon as a warship appeared over the horizon. Nor, in the days of *laissez faire* economics, were the courts inclined to favour the Admiralty, and several officers found themselves held personally liable for a wrongful arrest. However, the odious traffic was brought within limits, and of course the end of the American Civil War robbed West African slave-traders of their most lucrative market. Emphasis shifted to the east coast of Africa and the Persian Gulf, where a more ancient tradition of slave-owning persisted.

Above: A French drawing of the *frégate cuirassée* HMS *Bellerophon.*

Returning to the subject of technical change, the next big leap in naval technology was the adoption of iron. The British Industrial Revolution had been based on iron, and it is hardly surprising that shipbuilders wished to experiment in the new materials. By the 1830s there were a number of small iron craft, but navigation overseas was impossible until 1839, when a way of compensating for the effect of the iron hull on the magnetic compass could be found. As soon as this important improvement was made larger iron warships began to be laid down, but the art of metallurgy was in its infancy, and there were grave doubts about the effects of gunfire on an iron hull. A trial against the small iron steamer *Ruby* in 1846 showed that a lightly built iron hull offered no resistance to iron shot, but this was hardly surprising. A lengthier and more scientific series of trials by the gunnery training ship *Excellent* against various iron targets in 1849-1851 provided more serious evidence that iron ships were less resistant to damage than wooden ships.

Such pronouncements have caused later generations of historians to jeer at the 19th century Navy but there were good reasons for the adverse verdicts. Iron-

Left: A Naval Brigade landed from the battleship *Centurion*, typical of the landing forces used in small Victorian wars.

founding had not yet reached the stage where iron had sufficient elasticity to withstand the shock of a hit from a 78-lb cast-iron shot, and what worried the sailors of the 1840s was the way in which the iron was shredded into lethal splinters. Quality control was unknown, and there could be no guarantee that a batch of iron plates was of uniform quality.

The real problem was that the pace of technical advance was not accompanied by any practical experience. There was no major naval action anywhere in the world for nearly 40 years after Waterloo – the actions which did take place yielded no clues as to how wars of the future would be waged, for they were usually one-sided or involved nothing new. To cite one example, a pair of Texan sailing gun-brigs managed to defeat a Mexican squadron

Right: The single-screw two-decker HMS *London* in the 1860s, one of the last hybrid ships-of-the-line.

Below: HMS *Inflexible* had the largest muzzle-loading guns in the RN (16 inch) and was commanded by Fisher at the Bombardment of Alexandria in 1882.

Above: The China gunboat *Kinsha* (1909) was a converted Yangtze paddle steamer.

which included a British-built iron, steam-driven frigate. Such strange encounters tended to confuse the issue, and so it was not until 1854 that the Royal Navy's designers could know what was needed. That was the year in which the Crimean War broke out, but in fact the crisis was precipitated the year before, when the Russians annihilated a small Turkish squadron at Sinope.

In a rash fit of enthusiasm the French and British governments decided to retaliate against the Russians by sending an invasion force to the Crimea, in the vague hope that the soldiers could destroy the great arsenal at Sevastopol. Modern historians have by and large dealt mercilessly with the Crimean War, and even the

greatest English naval historian is on record as saying that the only reason the Royal Navy came out better than the Army was because the Army's incompetence plumbed unbelievable depths. But the facts do not support this, and the Royal Navy deserves considerable credit for the way in which it reacted to the challenge.

The real problem was not innate incompetence among the military but the grinding parsimony of successive governments, which had acted on the assumption that the country's armed forces were a wasting asset which would soon be reduced to minor policing duties. The Navy was in fact painfully trying to modernise its material on a slender budget, introducing not only steam but screw propulsion, and even the first primitive rifled shellguns. The first battleship built to take the screw propeller (as opposed to conversions) was launched in 1852. The Royal Dockyards still held vast stocks of seasoned timber, and so there was every financial reason to hold off the switch to iron construction as long as possible, although from the late 1830s an increasing amount of iron stiffening had been finding its way into large men o' war. It would be wrong, however, to deduce that the Royal

Navy had not modified its tactics since 1805, and no contemporary documents suggest that steam-driven ships of the line would ever fight under sail again. Sail was retained purely as an auxiliary form of power because steam engines were still so unreliable, and because they consumed so much coal on long voyages.

Above: HMS *Caesar*, one of Sir William White's famous *Majestic* class, the world's most powerful battleships when completed in the 1890s.

Below: Grand Harbour in Valletta, Malta c. 1909, with cruisers and battleships at their moorings.

Above: Searchlights were only part of the new electrical and hydraulic equipment which transformed the Navy in late Victorian times.

The opening shots of the Crimean War were fired against the forts around Sevastopol, and several ships were damaged by hits from Russian shells. The worst problem was that the big three- and two-deckers drew too much water to get in close, where their weight of gunfire could silence the forts, and as the forts could retaliate with red-hot shot as well as shells the ships were liable to be set on fire. Some sort of antidote was required, and both French and British took urgent steps to find the answer. The Royal Navy immediately embarked on the construction of small shallow-draught gunboats and mortar boats which could get in close, and the French proposed to build floating batteries. The first proposal was to protect them from shellfire by packing their sides with cannonballs, but the Royal Navy's designers suggested that 4-inch wrought iron armour plates would be better. Both navies agreed to build a number as quickly as possible, and the first three French floating batteries reached the Black Sea in time to take part in the bombardment of the fortress of Kinburn at the mouth of the Dnieper near Odessa. They made a tremendous impression, being hit repeatedly by shot and shell without suffering serious damage, and the case for armour plating was proved beyond doubt.

There was also the mundane question of logistics, and it is in this respect that the Navy showed its efficiency. The fleets that were sent initially to the Black Sea and the Baltic were largely sailing ships, although each ship of the line was allocated a smaller steamer to act as a tender and to tow her in and out of action, but by the following spring all of them had been replaced by steamships. This threw a great strain on maintenance, but a special

'steam factory' or repair ship was converted and sent to Balaclava. Similarly the need to provide fresh bread for the troops around Sevastopol was met by commissioning a 'steam bakery ship'. Despite the world-wide cholera pandemic, which decimated the Allied armies in the Crimea, the Navy's sick-list was much lower, and throughout the dreadful winter of 1854-55 which all but destroyed Lord Raglan's army, the Navy provided considerable help. A sawmill was set up at Balaclava to provide the soldiers with firewood, roasting ovens were improvised to enable the soldiers to roast their green coffee beans, and gradually the stinking quagmire that was Balaclava was turned into an efficient port. The wounded were kept on board warships until such time as Florence Nightingale could get a forward hospital established, and contemporary accounts reveal that the Navy had a grasp of basic hygiene which seemed to be lacking in the Army.

The Baltic Fleet acquitted itself well, although it had the less rewarding task of blockading the Russian Fleet in Kronstadt. In 1855 the new gunboats and mortar boats were used to mount a massive bombardment of Sveaborg, and had hostilities not ended in the following spring there were ambitious plans to use the floating batteries to support amphibious operations against Kronstadt and St Petersburg. Around Sveaborg the Royal Navy came up against the first modern sea mines, when HMS *Merlin* was damaged, and within a week or two a crude system of minesweeping had been devised.

There were, of course, many cobwebs to be swept out after the Crimean War, and the Navy had no grounds for complacency. The most worrying problem was still manpower, and in 1854 there had even been talk of resorting to impressment. The real answer was to give the seaman the same sort of commitment to long-term employment as the officers had enjoyed – what inducement was there to serve in a Navy which dismissed you at the end of each commission? There was also the problem of how to get rid of superannuated officers, who were not subject to retirement. The Navy List was swollen by aged veterans of the Napoleonic Wars, all of them in order of seniority but only a fraction having any hope of employment. In 1854 the Admiralty had been faced with an alarming shortage of 'young' flag-officers suited to command the overseas expeditions, and had to choose between the septuagenarian admirals and the octagenarians. There was an awful moment when command of the Baltic Fleet might have gone to the senior flag-officer, who was in his 90s. Even Nelson would have had to wait until 1844 to be-

The steam corvette *Royalist* at Dunedin, New Zealand, one of many masted cruisers.

come a full Admiral, for he could not overtake his contemporary Charles Nugent, posted as a Captain in 1779, just before him. The absurdity of the situation was finally resolved after the Crimean War by a wholesale 'purge', particularly of the swollen lists of half-pay lieutenants, giving them retirement pay in place of half-pay. Finally in 1870 the reform was completed by listing separate 'Active' and 'Retired' categories of officers on the Navy List. Along with the institution of long-term enlistment for seamen, it was a major step towards the creation of a modern navy.

Returning to technical developments, the brief alliance with the French did not survive long, and by 1859 the somewhat unstable regime of the Emperor Napoleon III was stoking the fires of Anglo-French naval rivalry once more. France was blessed with one of the most talented naval architects of his generation, Dupuy de Lôme, and he showed that it was possible to build an 'ironclad' frigate, with the same protection against gunfire as the floating batteries of Kinburn and in addition the ability to steam across the oceans. Her name, *la Gloire*, reflected national pride, and she was certainly a notable technical achievement, but when French newspapers started to talk of humbling British pride and vanquishing the Royal Navy British suspicions were aroused. For a time the government of the day dithered, airing schemes for cutting down and armouring all the wooden three-deckers, but eventually it reacted with a devastating counterstroke. Using Britain's vastly superior industrial resources, the Admiralty launched two ironclads of their own, the *Warrior* and the *Black Prince*. They were not only technically superior in being built entirely of iron (as opposed to the wooden hull of the *Gloire*) but were also larger, faster and more heavily armed. Known as the 'black snakes of the Channel' from their sleek, black hulls, the two ironclads were merely the forerunners of a large programme which rapidly closed the gap opened up between the Royal Navy and the French, and the invasion scare of 1859 was soon forgotten. But the industrial race was only just beginning, and within a very short time even the *Warrior* and the *Gloire* looked old-fashioned. Inventors and industrialists produced bigger guns and improved armour, while engineers produced revolving turrets or cupolas to do away with the traditional broadside disposition of guns.

In 1862 the Admiralty ordered its first turret ship, the *Prince Albert*, a far-sighted decision which was endorsed by the Battle of Hampton Roads in March that year. The advantage of the turret was that it provided all-round fire, and enabled gunpower to be increased without an expensive increase in size. There were other solutions to the problem, such as the central battery, and for a decade a 'Fleet of Samples' was built, conforming to every whim of the designer. Eventually, however, the ferment subsided, and with the completion of HMS *Devastation* in 1873 the modern battleship began to emerge. What made her so revolutionary was the fact that she was 'mastless'; in short, she was intended to fight under steam alone. It was the formal admission that the age of the sailing warship was over. Warships would continue to be given auxiliary sails for another ten years, but only to save coal on long passages, and not for manoeuvring in action.

In one respect the Royal Navy could be accused of being excessively cautious and conservative. Up to the late 1850s the muzzle-loading smooth-bore gun had dominated, with only slight competition from a series of experimental rifled guns, but in 1858 the Royal Navy followed the lead of the French and adopted breech-loading guns. The move was premature, however, for the Armstrong gun had several glaring faults. Accidents during the bombardment of Kagoshima in Japan in 1863 caused a public scandal and the Armstrong gun was hastily withdrawn – to appease the very Press and Parliamentary pressure which had forced the Navy to buy it three years earlier. As a result of the scandal the Navy reverted to muzzle-loaders, but retained the Armstrong principle of building up the strength by hoops of iron. It was a logical reaction but official inertia resulted in the retention of muzzle-loaders for another 20 years, long after every other front-rank navy had changed. Despite the Royal Navy being the Senior

Below: The 'dreadnought armoured cruiser' HMAS *Australia* fitting out in 1912.

Service its guns were obtained from the British Army, whose main gun-foundry, the Arsenal at Woolwich, remained a by-word for inefficiency throughout this period.

The worst problem afflicting the Royal Navy during the 1870s and 1880s was the lack of any serious strategic thought among the officer corps. It was felt that the subject of naval strategy could be safely left to flag-officers, and little attempt was made to foster any sort of analytical thought about how the Royal Navy might function in time of war. Lack of action was not the problem, for the Navy was constantly involved in minor actions around the world. The enforcement of *Pax Britannica* meant that a constant burden of responsibility was laid on the shoulder of junior officers; they could be called on to lead raids against slavers in West Africa, boat-actions against pirates off Borneo, or bombard a shore position. It was an age of colonial expansion among all advanced European nations, but only Britain had a navy big enough to provide world-wide protection to traders and travellers. It came to be known as 'gunboat diplomacy' because the smallest seagoing command was a gunboat; from the fact that they were usually commanded by lieutenants came the rank of Lieutenant-in-command, the modern Lieutenant-Commander.

The problem with so much activity was that a whole generation of officers came to believe that the Royal Navy was destined by Providence to be the world's police-man. Ships came to be designed primarily for cruising on foreign stations rather than to fight French and Russian ships, and as a result it came as an unpleasant shock at the beginning of the 1880s to realise that not only the French and Russians but other nations like the Italians and Germans had begun to benefit from their own industrial revolutions. The days when Great Britain had enjoyed a monopoly of high technology were gone, and henceforward she would have to fight to retain her position in the world. It was all the more important to

modernise the Royal Navy, and from then on progress was ever-more rapid. The old Surveyor's Department was replaced by the Director of Naval Construction's Department, the Navy won back control of its guns and a new relationship with industry was forged, to make sure that industry was capable of meeting the Navy's needs at all times. Another important reform was the creation of a Naval Intelligence Department. Public interest in the Navy, which had flagged during the 1860s and 1870s, began to revive, and in September 1884 the influential *Pall Mall Gazette* ran a series of articles on 'The Truth About the Navy.' They had been written anonymously but everyone knew that the author was W T Stead at the instigation of H W Arnold Forster, a noted 'Big Navy' man. What was less obvious was that the technical points raised in the articles had been vetted by the Captain of the Gunnery School, HMS *Excellent*, one Captain John Fisher RN.

The Navy's critics were given more ammunition when it was revealed that during one of the periodic 'Russian War Scares' in the spring of 1885 ships had taken months to mobilise. In 1886 the election of a Conservative government reflected a new public mood of impatience. At the Jubilee Colonial Conference in 1887 the Prime Minister, Lord Salisbury, outlined the problem succinctly:

"The circumstances in which we live, and the tendencies of human nature as we know it, in all times of history teach that, where there is a liability to attack, and defencelessness, attack will come. The English colonies comprise some of the richest and most desirable portions of the earth's surface. The desire for foreign and colonial possessions is increasing among the nations of Europe. The power of concentrating naval and military force is increasing under the influence of scientific progress. Put all these things together and you will see that the Colonies have a real and genuine interest in the shield which

their imperial connection throws over them, and that they have a ground for joining with us in making the defence of the Empire effective.'

One last scare was needed to force the Government's hand. Early in 1889 Parliament received the Report on the Annual Manoeuvres of the previous year, and it came to the unpalatable conclusion that the Fleet was 'altogether inadequate to take the offensive in a war with only one Great Power.' Two things emerged from this report, the formulation of the 'Two-Power Standard', a governing principle that the Royal Navy should be maintained at a strength equal to any two potential enemies, and a firm resolve by the majority of Conservatives and Liberals that the Navy must be strengthened urgently. On 7th March 1889, Lord George Hamilton introduced the Naval Defence Bill, providing for 70 new warships to be built in five years, at a cost of £21,500,000 – 8 1st Class battleships, 2 2nd Class battleships, 9 1st Class cruisers, 29 2nd Class cruisers, 4 3rd Class cruisers and 18 torpedo gunboats.

The benefits of the recent reforms were soon obvious. Under the supervision of the Director of Naval Construction, Sir William White, the Royal Dockyards were not only overhauled but were now as efficient as any private shipyard in the country. Portsmouth Dockyard built the lead-ship of the *Royal Sovereign* class, the new 1st Class battleships, in less than three years. Portsmouth and Chatham Dockyards raced to finish No. 1 and No. 2 of the next class, the *Majestic* and *Magnificent*; the respective building times of 22 months and 24 months were both world records. Nor were these ships famous simply because they were built quickly, for the *Royal Sovereign*s were magnificent seaboats, well-armed, fast and handsome. In the words of Oscar Parkes, White had 'provided the Navy with the finest group of fighting ships afloat ... for the first time since the

Devastation set a new standard for unsightliness, a British battleship presented a proud, pleasing and symmetrical profile which was unmatched by any other warship afloat . . .'

White already had the reputation of being the greatest living warship-designer, and is still regarded as the greatest British naval architect. His next creation, the nine *Majestic* Class battleships built between 1894 and 1898, were even better than the *Royal Sovereign*s, and became the model for other navies. In essence they were not improved upon for another ten years, apart from minor details, and they were still rendering sterling service in the First World War on subsidiary duties.

The Naval Defence Act was the opening shot in a European naval arms race that was to gather momentum steadily, through the 1890s and on into the 20th century. But the traditional enemies, France and Russia, were slowly but surely being edged aside by a brash newcomer, Germany. In 1898 a dispute with France over the Sudan nearly led to war, but within five years the mutual distrust and fear of Germany led the two traditional foes to join an *Entente*, and the destruction of

Russia's military might by the Japanese in 1904 removed her from the board. In the meantime, however, Tirpitz had steered the First Navy Law through the Reichstag, and the passage of the Second Navy Law in 1900 alerted British politicians to the new danger. The time had come for another shakeup, such as the one which preceded the Naval Defence Act, but this time the driving force would come from within the uniformed ranks of the Navy.

The man who would generate this cataclysmic change was Vice-Admiral Sir John Fisher, who had returned from commanding the Mediterranean Fleet in 1902 as Second Sea Lord. His career had already spanned a violent half-century, from the Crimean War to the Second China War and then to the bombardment of Alexandria in 1882. But his real claim to fame was as a technician, and from 1861 he had become a leading light, in both mine warfare and gunnery, rising rapidly under the patronage of enlightened superiors. In 1886 he became Director of Naval Ordnance and supervised the return of responsibility for naval guns from the Army back to the Navy, where it belonged, and in 1892 he was given the

Above: Crowds on the foreshore watch the 1911 Naval Review in Spithead.

influential post of Controller (Third Sea Lord). His most lasting gift to the Navy was undoubtedly a far-reaching reform of training and education, not just for officers but for the 'lower deck', but that side of Fisher's activities has been overshadowed by his intervention in shipdesign.

When Fisher returned from the Mediterranean he brought with him ideas for a new super-battleship, proposed to him by W H Gard, then Chief Constructor at Malta. Gard subsequently moved to Portsmouth, where he was able to provide Fisher with further designs such as 'HMS *Untakeable*', and so when Fisher became First Sea Lord in October 1904 much spadework had been done. He immediately established a Committee on Designs

Below: The new 'super dreadnoughts' *Iron Duke* and *Marlborough* (foreground) and three *King George V* class battleships arriving in Spithead for Test Mobilisation in July 1914.

under his chairmanship, to consider designs for new battleships and armoured cruisers, and by 13th January 1905 the details of a revolutionary new battleship were established.

The new ship, to be called *Dreadnought*, was a remarkable creation, displacing nearly 18,000 tons and armed with ten 12-inch guns. What distinguished her from previous battleships was the fact that she carried ten 12-inch guns (as against four in contemporaries) and apart from 24 light guns for repelling torpedo-boats, dispensed with the secondary armament of 6-inch guns which had been standard for many years. The reason for this startling increase in armament was the growing need to fire at long range, to keep out of range of torpedoes; at 7000 yards or more it was impossible to distinguish one shell-splash from another, and a uniform spread of 12-inch shell splashes offered a better chance to control gunfire. This was not an inspiration of Fisher but pressure from the gunnery branch of the Navy, and a reflection of pressures in other navies, particularly the American, who were planning to build two similar ships, armed with eight 12-inch guns. Where Fisher was clever was in laying down the *Dreadnought* at the beginning of October 1905 and building her at such speed that she was ready before any rivals.

The building of the *Dreadnought* established a record that has never been beaten, and it shows the extraordinary pitch of efficiency that the Royal Navy's Dockyards had reached since the 1880s. The ship was launched on 10th February 1906, just four months after her keel was laid, and on 3rd October 1906 she started preliminary basin trials. It was a piece of showmanship, of course, and the ship did not actually put to sea for another two months, but the building of an 18,000-ton prototype warship in 14 months was still a staggering feat. There had been considerable stage-management, using guns diverted from two other battleships and a great deal of pre-positioning of steel, but Fisher reckoned correctly that if there was to be an arms race with Germany it was better to be first.

There was another area in which the *Dreadnought* broke new ground, the adoption of the Parsons steam turbine. The Royal Navy had pioneered the use of the Parsons turbine in destroyers in 1900, and had subsequently built a small cruiser to test bigger installations, but nobody had yet dared to try turbines in a very large ship – not even the commercial shipbuilders. Fortunately this bold step was an unqualified success, and soon the world's battleships were following suit.

Fisher followed this coup with an even more revolutionary design for a '*Dreadnought* armoured cruiser' of roughly the same displacement but steaming at 25 knots as against 21. To achieve this one pair of 12-inch guns had to be dropped and side armour was thinned from 11 inches to only 6 inches, as in contemporary armoured cruisers. The prototype, HMS *Invincible*, went to sea in March 1908 and caused as big a sensation as the *Dreadnought*. Fisher turned his attention to destroyers as well, producing a new type of oil-fuelled destroyer capable of much higher speeds than her predecessors, for speed was one of Fisher's gods. He inspired men to enormous efforts with ruthless energy, handing down slogans such as, 'Only speed gives protection', 'Build first, build fast, each one better than the last.' He galvanized the Royal Navy's bureaucracy and above all, made officers and men aware that there would be a war with Germany.

In spite of all that he achieved modern historians see Fisher as a mixed blessing, and there are grounds for thinking that he did as much damage as good. His passion for slogans hid the fact that he really had very little grasp of the fundamentals of modern warfare, and his much vaunted ship-designs all contained major flaws. His beloved '*Dreadnought* armoured cruisers' were quickly promoted to 'battlecruisers' under the delusion that they were some sort of equivalent to a battleship, whereas their skimpy armouring made them quite unfit to fight battleships. His 'Tribal' Class destroyers were so short on fuel that when war came in 1914 they could only be allowed to serve in the English Channel, and his detestation of cruisers left the Navy very short of them. True, he was a passionate advocate of submarines, but because he saw them as a substitute for what he scorned as the 'defensive' use of mines, he built large numbers for harbour and coastal defence, too small for use across the North Sea.

The worst thing that Fisher did to his beloved Navy was to divide its officers into the 'Fishpond' of his favourites and toadies, and the 'Outer Darkness' of people who disagreed with him. Vindictiveness and ingratitude were hallmarks of Fisher's character, and many people had their naval careers unfairly blighted. Others were promoted for agreeing with the First Sea Lord, only to reveal their inadequacies in wartime. The problem was Fisher's strength of character, which tended to overwhelm lesser mortals and stifle debate. What finally enabled the Navy to survive the Fisher regime was the existence of a third body of opinion, neither in disgrace nor in the 'Fishpond', and determined to do their duty without getting involved in Navy politics.

Above right: The submarine *D.3* in a floating dock at Harwich in 1915, alongside the salvaged submarine minelaying U-Boat *UC.2*.

Below right: The battleship *Monarch* (1910) and her sisters reintroduced the 13.5 inch gun.

Below: HMS *Tipperary* was ordered by Chile but was taken over by the Royal Navy in 1914 and served as a flotilla leader at Jutland.

The last moments of the *Scharnhorst* and *Gneisenau* at the Battle of the Falklands in November 1914.

World War I

The war which Fisher constantly foretold finally broke out in August 1914, and on paper the Royal Navy was at its peak. Its strength in ships was more than adequate to maintain the Two-Power Standard:

- 20 dreadnought battleships in commission
- +13 completing or under construction
- 8 dreadnought battlecruisers
- +1 completing
- 40 'pre-dreadnought' battleships
- 37 old light cruisers
- 34 modern light cruisers
- +16 completing or under construction
- 31 large cruisers
- 112 old destroyers
- 112 modern destroyers

In addition the Admiralty could count on an additional Australian battlecruiser as well as modern light cruisers and destroyers, and just before the outbreak of hostilities two Turkish dreadnoughts were seized and commissioned as HMS *Agincourt* and HMS *Erin*.

In material respects the Royal Navy was ready, and thanks to the young First Lord of the Admiralty, Winston Churchill, the Fleet was fully mobilized before war actually broke out. As soon as the news from Sarajevo came through he cancelled leave for the crews of the ships which had just taken part in a test mobilization.

In other respects the Royal Navy was, however, not well equipped. The education of officers was still inadequate, with little scope for initiative and little encouragement to think about the purpose of wartime operations. Nor were the higher echelons of the service well trained in their profession. Against the wishes of Fisher and the senior admirals Winston

Churchill had begun the long overdue task of creating a Naval Staff, and because this organisation was in its infancy all the Royal Navy's wartime operations were to be marred by sloppy or downright incompetent staffwork. Officers and men were brave and well disciplined, but all too often there was little or no initiative.

There was also the problem that the British public had been led to believe that a naval war in the North Sea would be a brisk campaign of three or four weeks, culminating in a second Battle of Trafalgar. Little attention had been paid to the real lessons of history, which taught that victory had only followed after another ten years of hard campaigning. Even the German Navy fell into the trap of thinking that the British would immediately institute a close blockade of their ports, laying their ships open to attack from U-Boats and torpedo-craft. Instead the newly formed Grand Fleet (a revival of the old Elizabethan term) vanished into the mists of the North Sea, and was not seen for many months. Its new base was Scapa Flow, a huge natural anchorage in the Orkneys, far to the north but ideally situated to block the exit into the Atlantic. Close surveillance was to be left to submarines and light surface forces. Both sides had greatly exaggerated the willingness of the opposition to take risks, and so the expected pre-emptive attacks did not materialise. However on 28th August the British launched an ill-coordinated attack on the German light forces in the Heligoland Bight which resulted in the sinking of three light cruisers. The staffwork was abysmally poor, with various groups of British ships milling around the Bight with

no idea of each others' presence, but in spite of a number of close shaves nobody fired on a friendly ship and the raiders withdrew at the end of the morning without serious casualties.

The Royal Navy spent nearly two years patrolling the North Sea before it could bring the main German High Seas Fleet to action. Scapa Flow was over 500 miles away from the main German base at Wilhelmshaven, and so isolated detachments had little difficulty in mounting hit-and-run raids on the English coast, bombarding coastal towns like Scarborough and Hartlepool. Public opinion was outraged, but there was little that the Commander-in-Chief, Sir John Jellicoe, could do to counter such pinprick raids, and interception depended on early warning and a pinch of luck.

Fortunately British intelligence was first-class, and as early as October 1914 the cryptanalysts of Room 40 at the Admiralty had a copy of the German code-book, recovered by the Russians from the wreck of the light cruiser *Magdeburg*. Before long two more code-books were in Room 40's possession, giving the British a priceless advantage, one which they were not to lose for the rest of the war. The primitive state of the Naval Staff organisation prevented the Grand Fleet from reaping the full benefit, for Room 40 was not permitted to correlate its intercepts and decrypts with operational plans. Indeed the Director of the Operations Division, Captain Jackson, held Room 40 in great contempt, and showed little understanding of the value of intelligence in modern warfare.

Eventually Vice-Admiral Sir David

Above right: The *Birmingham* was typical of the latest British light cruisers, fast, weatherly and well armed.

Below: The *Royal Oak* leads the *Hercules* (right) in the line of battle at Jutland.

H.MS. BIRMINGHAM

Beatty and the Battle-Cruiser Squadron, comprising the *Lion, Tiger, Princess Royal, New Zealand* and *Indomitable*, were able to bring the German battle-cruisers under Admiral Hipper to action in the Battle of the Dogger Bank in January 1915. Although it looked as if Hipper had blundered into a trap he was allowed to escape comparatively lightly after a signal from the British flagship was misinterpreted. Instead of pursuing the enemy battlecruisers all the British ships turned to attack the crippled armoured cruiser *Blucher*, and by the time the muddle could be sorted out it was too late. Beatty quite rightly treated it as a failure, for his ships could and should have sunk at least one major unit such as the *Seydlitz*.

Outside home waters there was also a measure of disappointment. The expected German onslaught on shipping proved much less dangerous than expected, although Vice-Admiral Spee's cruiser squadron did manage to destroy two elderly armoured cruisers off Coronel on the coast of Chile in October 1914. It came as a severe shock after a century of

uncontested mastery of the sea, but the Admiralty reacted swiftly by sending the battlecruisers *Invincible* and *Inflexible* to the Falkland Islands. They arrived just in time to prevent the capture of Port Stanley, and next day put to sea and sank all but one of Spee's ships in the Battle of the Falklands. The light cruiser *Emden* remained at large for some time, leading a charmed life by altering her appearance, but finally the Australian cruiser HMAS *Sydney* caught her trying to cut the international telegraph cable at Cocos-Keeling Island in the Pacific. The *Königsberg* was forced to take shelter in the Rufiji River in East Africa, and various mercantile auxiliaries were all sunk or interned, without having inflicted more than 1 per cent loss on the huge British merchant fleet.

The only way in which the German Navy could make any lasting impression on the British was to use its U-Boats. As early as September 1914 a single U-Boat had torpedoed three old armoured cruisers in the North Sea, but there had been no attempt to attack merchant shipping, apart from a few isolated incidents. The reason was that International Law forbade the sinking of merchantmen without first examining their papers and sending the

crew to safety or taking them prisoner. Of course a 500-ton submarine could not accommodate prisoners, and could not even accommodate the extra prize-crews needed to take enemy ships into a friendly port, but the laws and customs governing war against commerce had been drawn up in the days when all commerce-raiders were surface ships.

Inevitably both German submarine commanders and the admirals began to ignore the restrictions, and by the end of January 1915 ten merchantmen had been sunk, most of them without warning. Faced with such a tempting array of targets German military opinion pressed for an abandonment of the 'Prize Law', even if it meant offending neutral opinion. On 4th February 1915 Germany declared the waters around the British Isles to be a 'War Zone' in which all ships would be destroyed. The new policy was most effective, and the waters around the British Isles became highly dangerous to shipping. The climax of the campaign was the torpedoing of the liner *Lusitania* in April, but it had the effect of mobilising American public opinion against Germany to such an extent that in August the 'unrestricted' campaign had to be stop-

ped. It had, however, cost the British 748,000 tons of shipping.

The British had lost sight of a fundamental truth: their lines of communication stretched across the Atlantic, not across the Channel to France, and the more men and munitions they sent to France the more they depended on that transatlantic lifeline. Everybody had thought that the war would be 'over by Christmas' and so all work on merchant shipbuilding had been stopped to allow warships to be built. There was no salvage organisation to recover damaged ships and no provision to repair them, so the priceless asset of merchant shipping was being expended without replacement. To make matters worse the British undertook

world-wide commitments, sending troops
to East Africa, West Africa, and Egypt, and
agreed to supply their allies with the
necessities of war. All this was taking
place against a backdrop of massive military operations in France and Belgium,
requiring enormous quantities of raw
materials to be imported.

Room 40 gave the Grand Fleet its big
chance to destroy the High Seas Fleet in
May 1916, for although the new German
C-in-C, Admiral Scheer, hoped to lure the
British into a U-Boat trap, a good two days
earlier decodes alerted the Admiralty to a
major German operation. At noon on 30th
May 1916 Admirals Jellicoe and Beatty
were warned that the High Seas Fleet
would probably put to sea early on the

Above: The destroyer *Scorpion* lying off the
Gallipoli beaches in 1915.

Left: The light cruiser *Canterbury*, developed
for working with destroyers, from the pre-war
Arethusa design.

Below: The 4th Flotilla of 'K' class destroyers in
the Solent in the summer of 1914.

Far left: Admiral Sir David Beatty, who later became Commander-in-chief of the Battle Cruiser Force.

Left: Rear Admiral the Hon. Horace Hood, who lost his life in the *Invincible*.

Contact was made by accident, when both sides sent light forces to investigate a small neutral ship which was blowing off steam. Shots were exchanged but both groups broke off to take the vital news to their flagships that the enemy was in sight. The rival battlecruisers engaged, six under Beatty against five under Hipper, but the odds shortened when HMS *Indefatigable* and HMS *Queen Mary* blew up after shell-hits. Beatty had four new fast battleships of the *Queen Elizabeth* class in support but they had been left behind (yet another signalling error by Beatty's flag-lieutenant), and took some time to catch up. The fire from their 15-inch guns helped to redress the balance for the Germans had only 11-inch and 12-inch guns, which were outranged, but the British force was gradually being drawn into battle with the main High Seas Fleet, exactly as Scheer had planned. However he had no idea that Beatty was playing the same game, and the British battlecruisers now drew away to the north, with the Germans in hot pursuit. At about 6.00 pm a German destroyer reported seeing 'about 60 ships' nearby, the first warning to Scheer that he was the one who had fallen into the trap.

Jellicoe had achieved everything that he could desire, with one exception. He

following day. At 5.40 pm the same afternoon the Grand Fleet weighed anchor and steamed out of Scapa Flow, more than 150 ships in the mightiest concentration of sea power yet seen:
Fleet Flagship: *Iron Duke*
1st Division, 2nd Battle Squadron: *Ajax, Centurion, Erin, King George V*
2nd Division, 2nd Battle Squadron: *Orion, Monarch, Conqueror, Thunderer*
3rd Division, 4th Battle Squadron: *Iron Duke, Royal Oak, Superb, Canada*
4th Division, 4th Battle Squadron: *Benbow, Bellerophon, Temeraire, Vanguard*
5th Division, 1st Battle Squadron: *Colossus, Collingwood, Neptune, St Vincent*
6th Division, 1st Battle Squadron: *Marlborough, Revenge, Hercules, Agincourt*
3rd Battle Cruiser Squadron: *Invincible, Inflexible, Indomitable*
1st Cruiser Squadron: *Defence, Warrior, Duke of Edinburgh, Black Prince*
2nd Cruiser Squadron: *Minotaur, Hampshire, Cochrane, Shannon*
4th Light Cruiser Squadron: *Calliope, Constance, Caroline, Royalist, Comus*
Light cruisers attached to 3rd Battle Cruiser Squadron: *Boadicea, Blanche, Bellona, Active, Canterbury, Chester*
4th Destroyer Flotilla: 18 destroyers
11th Destroyer Flotilla: 1 light cruiser and 15 destroyers
12th Destroyer Flotilla: 16 destroyers
Battle Cruiser Flagship: *Lion*
1st Battle Cruiser Squadron: *Princess Royal, Queen Mary, Tiger*
2nd Battle Cruiser Squadron: *New Zealand, Indefatigable*
5th Battle Cruiser Squadron: *Barham, Valiant, Warspite, Malaya*
1st Light Cruiser Squadron: *Galatea, Phaeton, Inconstant, Cordelia*

2nd Light Cruiser Squadron: *Southampton, Birmingham, Nottingham, Dublin*
3rd Light Cruiser Squadron: *Falmouth, Yarmouth, Birkenhead, Gloucester*
1st Destroyer Flotilla: 1 light cruiser, 9 destroyers
9th and 10th Destroyer Flotillas: 8 destroyers
13th Destroyer Flotilla: 1 light cruiser, 10 destroyers
In addition there was a seaplane carrier, HMS *Engadine*, and two destroyers, one acting as tender to the Fleet Flagship and one minelayer.

Against this fleet the Germans could muster 101 ships, including sixteen dreadnought battleships, five battlecruisers, six old pre-dreadnoughts, eleven light cruisers and seven flotillas of destroyers and torpedo boats.

Above right: The battlecruiser *Indefatigable*, minutes before she blew up in the opening phase of the Battle of Jutland.

Right: British shells fall near a flotilla of German torpedo boats as they attack the British battle line.

Below: As the Grand Fleet completes its deployment HMS *Superb* opens fire, with the *Canada* astern.

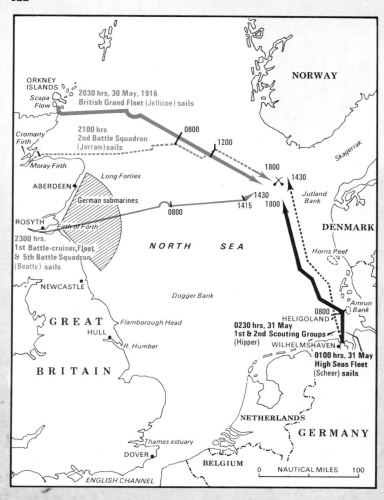

2030 hrs, 30 May, 1916
British Grand Fleet (Jellicoe) sails

2100 hrs
2nd Battle Squadron
(Jerram) sails

2300 hrs,
1st Battle-cruiser Fleet
& 5th Battle Squadron
(Beatty) sails

German submarines

ORKNEY ISLANDS
Scapa Flow
Cromarty Firth
Moray Firth
ABERDEEN
Long Forties
ROSYTH
Firth of Forth
NEWCASTLE
Dogger Bank
Flamborough Head
HULL
R. Humber
GREAT BRITAIN
Thames estuary
DOVER
ENGLISH CHANNEL
BELGIUM
NETHERLANDS
NORTH SEA
NORWAY
Skagerrak
Jutland Bank
DENMARK
Horns Reef
Amrun Bank
HELIGOLAND
WILHELMSHAVEN
GERMANY

0800
1200
1800
1430
1430
0800
1415
1800
0800

0230 hrs, 31 May
1st & 2nd Scouting Groups
(Hipper)

0100 hrs, 31 May
High Seas Fleet
(Scheer) sails

0   NAUTICAL MILES   100

was able to deploy his battle squadrons into line of battle, placing them between Scheer and the German line of retreat, but it was now late in the day. Not only was the day misty but the dense clouds of coal-smoke added to the murk, so that ships had great difficulty in identifying targets and signals. The Grand Fleet accomplished a masterly deployment, although another battlecruiser, HMS *Invincible*, was sunk by gunfire during this phase of the action. Twice the British crossed the German 'T', the tactical manoeuvre which should have ensured destruction of the German Fleet, but each time the Germans were able to make a turn away which was undetected in the bad light. Finally the two fleets drew apart as darkness fell, but Jellicoe had every reason to hope for a decisive battle at first light.

The Germans were in a bad position, trapped with the Grand Fleet straddling their escape route, but Scheer knew that his ships were all well equipped and trained for night-fighting and he decided to force a way through the light forces guarding the rear of the Grand Fleet. The gamble paid off, for the British had not trained for night-fighting, and their captains had not appreciated the importance of sending all sighting reports to the flagship. To make matters worse the Admiralty neglected to send Jellicoe a decoded German signal asking for an air-

Above left: A huge column of smoke hides the spot where HMS *Queen Mary* has just blown up.

Above right: The battlecruiser action, the first phase of the battle.

Right: The German High Seas Fleet deploying, demonstrating how quickly coal-smoke could reduce visibility.

Below: The destroyer *Badger* looking for survivors from the *Invincible*. The ends of the ship are resting on the Jutland Bank.

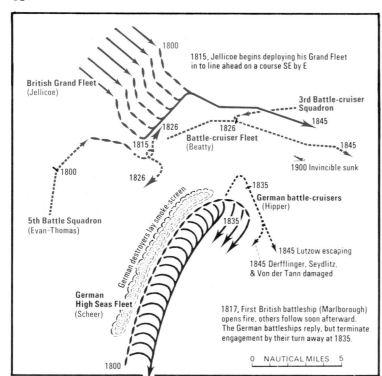

1815, Jellicoe begins deploying his Grand Fleet in to line ahead on a course SE by E

British Grand Fleet
(Jellicoe)

3rd Battle-cruiser Squadron

1845

1826

Battle-cruiser Fleet
(Beatty)

1845

1815

1826

1826

1800

1826

1900 Invincible sunk

1835

German battle-cruisers
(Hipper)

5th Battle Squadron
(Evan-Thomas)

1835

1845 Lutzow escaping

1845 Derfflinger, Seydlitz,
& Von der Tann damaged

German destroyers lay smoke-screen

German High Seas Fleet
(Scheer)

1817, First British battleship (Marlborough)
opens fire, others follow soon afterward.
The German battleships reply, but terminate
engagement by their turn away at 1835.

1800

0 NAUTICAL MILES 5

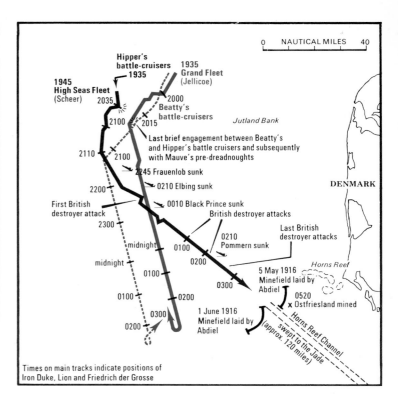

0 NAUTICAL MILES 40

Hipper's battle-cruisers
1935

1945
High Seas Fleet
(Scheer)

1935
Grand Fleet
(Jellicoe)

2035

2000
Beatty's battle-cruisers

Jutland Bank

2100

2015

2110

2100

Last brief engagement between Beatty's
and Hipper's battle cruisers and subsequently
with Mauve's pre-dreadnoughts

2200

2245 Frauenlob sunk

0210 Elbing sunk

First British
destroyer attack

0010 Black Prince sunk

British destroyer attacks

2300

DENMARK

Last British
destroyer attacks

midnight

0100

0210
Pommern sunk

0200

5 May 1916
Minefield laid by
Abdiel

Horns Reef

midnight

0100

0200

0300

0520
Ostfriesland mined

0100

0200

1 June 1916
Minefield laid by
Abdiel

Horns Reef Channel
swept to the Jade
(approx. 120 miles)

0200

0300

Times on main tracks indicate positions of
Iron Duke, Lion and Friedrich der Grosse

ship to reconnoitre a specific route back to Germany. Scheer's luck held, and his battered ships were nearing the swept channel through the minefields of Wilhelmshaven by 3.00 the next morning. He had lost a battlecruiser, a pre-dreadnought battleship and three light cruisers as against three battlecruisers and three armoured cruisers on the British side, and could claim a victory in material terms. But as an American commentator put it, the High Seas Fleet had escaped from gaol and assaulted its gaoler, but was back behind bars. Claims are still made that Germany won the Battle of Jutland, as it was named (from the Danish province of Jutland) but the real answer must surely be that the Royal Navy failed to win it, for the Grand Fleet, in spite of all its weaknesses in organisation and material, could have won a victory as magnificent as Trafalgar, and its failure to do so sounded the death-knell of British supremacy in the world. Worse, it condemned the Allies to another two years of bloody fighting on the Western Front, trying to remedy the deficiencies of sea power.

The post-Jutland inquest was long and thorough. The loss of the three battle-cruisers turned out to be caused by cordite-flash; British cordite was unstable because of impurities not eliminated during manufacture. What was much more disappointing was the failure of the heavy armour-piercing shells, which had scored repeated hits on German ships but had broken up on striking armour, instead of penetrating into the vitals before exploding. Both problems, once identified, could be tackled vigorously, and ships were given improved protection to magazines, new cordite and new shells. The night-fighting organisation was completely overhauled and tactical training was reformed, but it was all too late, and the Grand Fleet would never get a second chance.

The High Seas Fleet got to sea again, but it was not prepared to face the Grand Fleet, and its morale declined steadily throught 1917 and 1918. Despairing of a victory in the North Sea, Scheer put his support behind moves to reintroduce unrestricted U-Boat warfare, and this very quickly revealed how vulnerable the British were. Losses climbed alarmingly and the Admiralty could do little to check them. Vast numbers of yachts, trawlers and drifters were conscripted into the Auxiliary Patrol but still the losses went up, until by the beginning of 1917 one ship in every four around the British Isles was being sunk. When the United States entered the war the Commander-in-Chief of US Naval Forces in Europe, Admiral W S

Above left: The sinking wreck of HMS *Indefatigable,* photographed from the *New Zealand* by a midshipman.

Left: The moment when the *Invincible's* main magazines exploded and broke her in two. The cause was unstable propellant.

Sims, was told by Jellicoe that there were only six weeks' food supplies left in Britain, and that the country would be forced to negotiate with Germany unless some miracle could be wrought.

The miracle was about to happen, for on 27th April Jellicoe grudgingly gave his approval for an experimental convoy to be run. The arguments against convoy had sounded very convincing, but finally the Royal Navy turned back to the oldest measure of trade-protection of all. The results were truly miraculous, for shipping losses sank from 25 per cent to around 1 per cent within weeks. What had not been realised was that convoy also offered the only hope of *attacking* U-Boats, for as soon as they approached convoys they laid themselves open to counterattack by

Above: The light cruiser *Southampton* licks her wounds after the battle.

the escorts. As the young U-Boat commander Karl Dönitz was to point out later, convoying emptied the seas of shipping; for long periods there were no targets, and when smoke was sighted on the horizon it heralded a tightly packed formation surrounded by warships.

Although 1917 saw the tide of U-Boat successes rolled back, in other ways 1917 was the worst year of the war for the Royal Navy. The deficiencies in the Grand Fleet

Below: The hopper barge *Slinger* was fitted with an experimental catapult to test new ways of launching aircraft.

Above: The lightcruiser *Cardiff* leads the High Seas Fleet to the surrender.

were still being made good, and it was too soon to think of challenging the High Seas Fleet until supplies of the new shells were available. There were also delays in the introduction of depth-charges and an efficient mine, so that the Royal Navy could not take the offensive in any area. Even a small skirmish in the Heligoland Bight in November 1917 proved that staff-work was still poor, and the gains were not as impressive as they had been in the same area in August 1914. But there was a significant improvement in one area: more aircraft were now going to sea in HM ships, some on flying platforms on gun

turrets and others from the first primitive aircraft carriers. Something was needed to offset the advantage the High Seas Fleet had from its Zeppelin airships. These giant dirigibles often spotted British ships at sea and gave away their positions in time for the German Fleet to avoid them, and both Beatty and Jellicoe knew that any means of destroying the Zeppelins would help to bring about another fleet action.

The provision of aircraft was divided between fighters like the Sopwith Pup, intended to shoot down Zeppelins, and reconnaissance aircraft to scout for enemy ships and to spot the fall of shot for the Grand Fleet's battleships. So confident was the Grand Fleet in the future of aircraft at sea that at the end of 1917 an order was placed for the world's first true aircraft

carrier, to be called the *Hermes*. She would not see service until after the war, but interim carriers could be provided by converting an ex-Italian liner and a comandeered Chilean battleship.

The final act in the North Sea drama was the surrender of the High Seas Fleet, an event without parallel in naval history. Throughout 1918 morale sagged lower and lower among the men cooped up in the battleships at Kiel and Wilhelmshaven. The best and brightest officers, petty officers and seamen had long since been drafted to U-Boats and torpedo boats, and their places had been taken by reservists and conscripts, who had never imbibed the tradition of naval discipline. The worst problem was the dearth of what today might be called 'middle management',

and without the leavening of seasoned
petty officers a dangerous gulf opened up
between the officers and their men. The
slow strangulation of Germany by the
British blockade meant shortages of food
for everyone, including soldiers and
sailors, and when the Allied armies began
to win huge successes in the second half
of 1918 the word 'Armistice' was heard for
the first time. When the crews of the
battleships found out that an operation
was being planned at the end of October
they rebelled against any idea of a death-
ride against the Grand Fleet to preserve
the honour of the officer corps. On the
night of 29th-30th October mutiny broke
out among the ships lying in Schillig
Roads, and Admiral Hipper was forced to
cancel the operation. Not surprisingly the
men in the U-Boats and torpedo boats dis-
dained to join their comrades from the
battleships, for they despised them as
idlers who had managed to have a quiet
war. An unfair judgement, but not un-
common in the Royal Navy also, and
Hipper was able to order U-Boats to fire on
their own ships unless the Red Flag was
hauled down.

One of the most important conditions of
the Armistice was that specified German
ships, including the modern surface ships
of the High Seas Fleet and all U-Boats, must
be surrendered. On 21st November the
entire Grand Fleet, as well as French warships and the US 6th Battle Squadron,
formed a double line, through which
steamed the rusty, sullen dreadnoughts of

Above right: The German surrender in the
Firth of Forth in November 1918.

Below: The might of the Grand Fleet at sea in
1917, led by the flagship *Queen Elizabeth*.

HMS LONDON

The pre-Dreadnought battleship *London*, seen at Dover in 1910, became a minelayer in 1918.

the Kaiser's *Hochseeflotte*. From there they went to the dreary wastes of Scapa Flow, where they remained while the victors wrangled over the peace conditions. Finally on 21st June 1919 the German crews scuttled their ships in Scapa Flow.

This necessarily brief summary of the Royal Navy's part in winning the First World War has not touched on its major operations in theatres outside the North Sea and the Atlantic. It would be very misleading to suggest that the Grand Fleet was the whole Royal Navy or that other campaigns were less important. The Navy's role in the Mediterranean and the Dardanelles was crucial, permitting the Allies to bring pressure to bear on Turkey and the Austro-Hungarian Empire. The Gallipoli Expedition began as a bold and imaginative attempt to mount an amphibious operation, and its failure can hardly be blamed on the Navy alone. In fact when the German General Staff came to consider the evacuation of Cape Helles in 1916 (in which only a minute fraction of the expected casualties were incurred) they concluded that such an evacuation would never be repeated.

British warships, including many ancient veterans of the Victorian Navy, served in humble capacities around the world, old cruisers escorting convoys, battleships giving up their 12-inch guns to arm shallow-draught monitors or even submarines shelling Turkish trains in the Sea of Marmora; but even this gigantic effort was to be eclipsed in the Second World War.

Left: A Sopwith Pup fighter on HMAS *Sydney's* launching platform.

Below: A typical throng of warships in Scapa Flow, the Grand Fleet's main base from 1914 to 1918.

Above right: British shipyards made prodigious efforts to build new warships.

Right: HMS *Swiftsure* was disarmed in 1916, for possible use in the blocking of Ostend.

The Locust Years

The five *King George V* class were the first battleships to be built for 15 years.

The scuttling of the German Fleet at Scapa Flow, although embarrassing to the British, was a blessing in disguise. The Allies had soon started to squabble over the spoils, and just who would get how much of the German Navy was one of a number of issues, so its removal from the scene avoided any outright quarrel. That left the Royal Navy still the largest in the world by a considerable margin, but the United States was determined to have a navy 'Second to None', and had started a vast building programme in 1916. The Japanese, having also done extremely well out of the war, were determined not to forfeit any of their gains in the Pacific. At least that was the way the admirals saw things, but they reckoned without the universal war-weariness and the new wave of idealism exemplified by President Woodrow Wilson. The President's idealism struck a chord throughout the world, the League of Nations would make war an impossibility, and the post-war generation took 'Never Again' as its slogan.

The navies of the world could not afford to be so sanguine, and while nobody in London, Washington or Paris wanted to see another ruinous arms race, statesmen admitted that they still needed their instruments of policy. The Royal Navy had to consider whether it could retain the Two-Power Standard or not. With a vast empire spread around the world Britain clearly hoped to be at least equal to any single naval power. As France, Japan and Italy had much smaller navies, and with Germany disarmed and Russia disemboweling herself by Bolshevism and civil

Above: The old cruiser *Suffolk* and the USS *Brooklyn* at Vladivostok in 1919, supporting operations against the Bolsheviks.

Far right: The 8-barrelled 2-pounder (40mm) pom-pom started development in 1921 as a defence against air attack.

Below: HMS *Eagle* was converted from the incomplete hull of a Chilean battleship. She tested many new aviation ideas in the early 1920s.

war, that left only the United States Navy as a serious rival. But Japan was desperately trying to catch up in order to extend her influence in the Pacific, for her rulers sensed that the high tide of white colonialism was receding. Although the Americans and British distrusted one another they distrusted the Japanese much more, and neither nation wished to see the Japanese exploiting the imbalance of power in the Pacific.

Under American pressure the British refused to renew the Anglo-Japanese Treaty, which had been negotiated nearly 20 years earlier to allow the British to withdraw forces from the Far East. To match the American 'Second to None' programme of 1916 the Japanese had initiated their own '8-8' programme of battleship-building, and were now prepared to spend enormous sums of money to expand the Imperial Navy. Tension in the Far East reached such a peak by 1920 that the Americans were warned diplomatically that if they fortified Cavite in the Philippines there would be war. Then the taxpayers began to have second thoughts about the huge fleet of battleships which was planned, and when the British announced in 1921 that if there was no reduction of rivalry they too would be forced to build large battleships, the American Government took the only sensible way out. The Secretary of State, Charles Evans Hughes, convened an International Naval Disarmament Conference in Washington at the end of 1921, and proposed what would today be called mutually balanced force reductions. He called for a ten-year moratorium on battleship-building, the

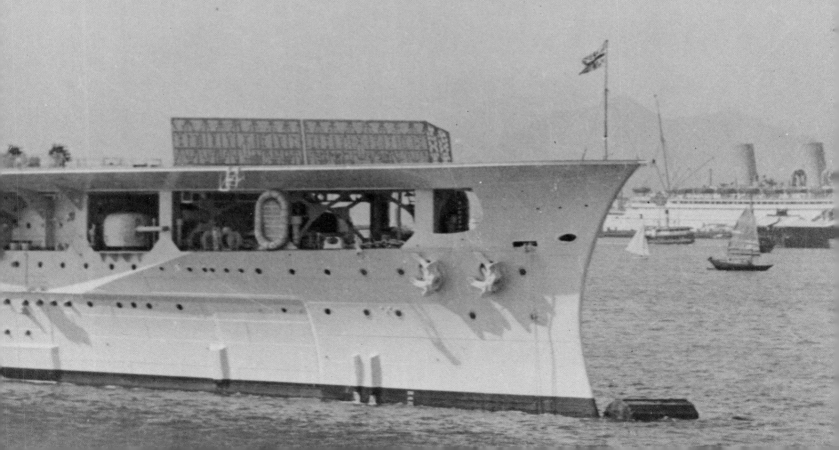

scrapping of older battleships, and above all, the cancellation of new construction.

The Americans were only too happy to cancel their unbuilt ships (although some diehard admirals protested) and the Japanese gave in with ill grace; the Royal Navy had already been told by the Cabinet that the ships would not be sanctioned in any case, but it still left the Royal Navy in a weak position. Apart from the new battlecruiser *Hood* and a quartet of light battlecruisers of very dubious fighting value, the Royal Navy had laid down no new battleships since 1914, and their largest gun was 15-inch calibre. In the interim the Americans and Japanese had both completed ships armed with the much more powerful 16-inch gun, which would outclass the British *Queen Elizabeth* and *Revenge* classes. The British also had the benefit of battle-experience, and wanted to build some modern capital ships which would incorporate all the lessons of Jutland, so they blocked all the proposals for a straightforward 'holiday' in battleship building unless the other countries agreed to scrap their most modern ships.

Finally a compromise was reached whereby the Americans kept three out of their four 16-inch gunned ships, the Japanese kept their two, and the British were allowed to build two 16-inch gunned ships to join the 15-inch gunned *Hood*.

Above: The new aircraft carrier *Ark Royal* in 1939.

Top right: HMS *Hermes*, the first carrier ever designed from the keel up.

Right: The unorthodox profile of the battleship *Nelson* (1927).

Below: Many of the 'V&W' class destroyers such as HMS *Walker*, survived to play an important role in World War II.

The ratio of American:British:Japanese strength was to be 5:5:3, an outcome which the Japanese denounced as a 'Rolls: Rolls:Ford' agreement, but they had little option but to sign, along with the French and Italians, who had an even smaller ratio than the Japanese. A new upper limit for battleships was established, 35,000 tons and 16-inch guns, while cruisers were limited to 10,000 tons and 8-inch guns. Germany's naval strength was fixed by the Treaty of Versailles, and she was only permitted to retain six old pre-dreadnought battleships; she was forbidden to own U-Boats. Nobody even bothered to ask the Soviet Union what she thought about international naval limitations.

Under the terms of the Washington Treaty, signed in 1922, the Royal Navy emerged as a shadow of its former self, reduced to 22 battleships and 70 cruisers, although two surplus light battlecruisers were allowed to be converted to aircraft carriers and two new battleships could be built. What hurt most was the abandonment of the Two-Power Standard but in retrospect it was no more than recognition of the fact that the British Empire was now bankrupt after the enormous cost of the war. Indeed later generations were to marvel that the British Empire was to last another 25 years, for it proved all but impossible to defend in 1941. The money simply could not be found to maintain a large fleet, and even vitally needed modernisation was deferred as long as possible in order to make the money go further. Many accusations have been hurled at the heads of the various Boards of Admiralty from 1922 onwards, most of them false, but one glaring failure stands out. While other navies, notably the United States, Japan and Italy, pressed ahead with modernisation schemes, even laying up quite a large percentage of their battleships, the British continued to keep a full battle fleet in commission. There was a blind faith in the *appearance* of the Royal Navy, and a quaint assumption that the withdrawal of, say, five battleships for re-armouring and modernisation would bring the Empire crashing down.

The two new battleships, named *Nelson* and *Rodney*, joined the Fleet in 1927, but thereafter no new construction could be started until 1932. A steady trickle of new cruisers and destroyers began to come forward to replace the worn-out First World War ships. The Washington Treaty tonnage limits, although somewhat unrealistic, had a beneficial effect in that they forced Admiralty designers to adopt new lighter methods of construction and more efficient machinery, and certainly most of the ships built in the 1920s and 1930s stood the test of battle. The main weakness was in anti-aircraft defence, although ironically the Royal Navy had pioneered the multi-barrelled anti-aircraft weapon as early as 1921, when the first design for a multiple pom-pom (later nicknamed the 'Chicago Piano') was drawn up. No money could be spared for the development of high-angle guns or the fire-control needed to make them effective, and Admiralty records reflect the concern throughout the period.

In one important respect, however, the Royal Navy was not merely under-equipped but actually slipping badly behind. In April 1918, as part of a wartime expedient, the Royal Naval Air Service handed over all its aircraft, with those of the Royal Flying Corps, to form the new independent Royal Air Force. This was hailed as the dawn of a new and radically different form of warfare, but the effect on the Royal Navy was disastrous, for at a stroke it lost all its youthful and vigorous air-minded officers. In theory the RAF would simply fly the aircraft off the Navy's carriers, but in practice the procurement

Right: The carrier *Furious* after reconstruction in 1919-22.

Below: Gun crew closed up in one of HMS *Orion*'s 6 inch gun turrets.

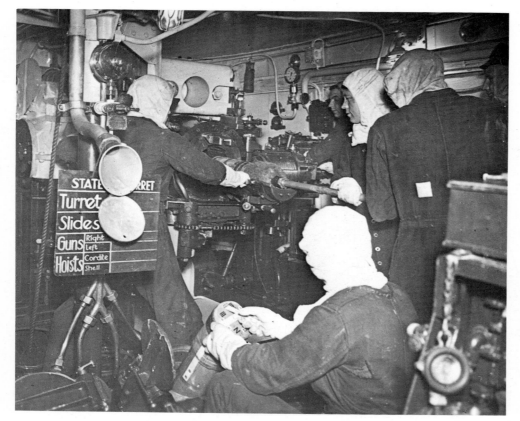

Below right: The cruiser HMS *Southampton*, designed to counter new Japanese cruisers.

of aircraft and the training of aircrew was kept firmly in Air Ministry hands.

Probably the biggest failure of this dual control was that the RAF did not provide the Navy with realistic exercises in air-defence, and because the higher echelons of the Air Force were obsessed by the concept of strategic bombing they paid little attention to maritime cooperation. Across the Atlantic the US Navy had not made that mistake, and its aviators were able to fight the battle for naval air power from within their service. More ominous for the British was the enthusiasm for naval air power shown by the Japanese. American and Japanese naval aircraft improved year by year, in step with land aircraft developments, whereas the Fleet Air Arm sported an ancient collection of slow and clumsy biplanes. Worse was the lack of any real appreciation of the potential of carrier warfare, although to be fair to the Admiralty, each year it raised the subject of recovering control of its own aviation, and as with everything else, lack of money was the

equally frequent excuse for retaining the existing system.

The RAF finally relinquished control of the Fleet Air Arm, not because it had seen the light but because in 1936 it did not want to spend any re-armament funds on naval aircraft. As it then withdrew its pilots and maintenance personnel it left the Fleet Air Arm in a desperate position, starting a large pilot-training programme and at the same time trying to draw up specifications for a completely new range of aircraft. It is that sorry state of affairs which accounts for the fact that the Fleet Air Arm's strike aircraft at the outbreak of war in 1939 was a 90mph biplane, at a time when contemporary American and Japanese naval aircraft were vastly superior.

The world-wide slump which followed the Wall Street crash had its effect on Great Britain, just as it did elsewhere, but indirectly it had a particular effect on the Royal Navy. Reeling under the pressure from the Treasury to cut public expenditure and to cope with a loss of confidence in sterling, the Government set up an Economy Committee early in 1931. This committee demanded every Department of State to submit its proposals for cost-cutting, and was even looking for cuts in rates of pay, so grave was the national emergency. The Board of Admiralty protested rather weakly that certain rates of pay awarded to ratings in 1919 had virtually been guaranteed (the 1919 rates had been intended to offset wartime inflation), but that the sailors concerned would, no doubt, accept a reduction of pay if it was shared by other employees of the Crown. In what followed the Admiralty showed remarkably little sensitivity, for the Press continued to debate the subject of National Economies but no attempt was made to set the men's minds at rest about the state of negotiations. The Treasury did not want the Fleet told until the matter had been aired in Parliament, but even after that a series of administrative blunders prevented a number of ships and bases from receiving any official statement about pay-cuts. When it was learned that pay-cuts for the police, for example, had been deferred because of the threat that the police would strike, the deepest suspicions of the sailors were confirmed, that they alone would have to make the sacrifice.

The upshot of all this backstairs activity was that an official Admiralty letter was issued on 10th September 1931, to be read on board HM ships. It was not, in the words of Captain Roskill, 'happily worded', and its reception was not friendly, for it was clear that the cuts would be felt unevenly, and that their effect for some men would be extremely harsh. The worst example would be an Able Seaman (AB) on the 1919 rate, whose basic pay would fall from four shillings (20 pence) per day to three shillings, a cut of 25 per cent. Specialist pay and allowances

could make a difference to the basic pay, but to the men it was the basic rate which mattered most.

On the night of Sunday 13th September reports came through of disturbances at Invergordon, where the Atlantic Fleet was about to begin exercises. It seems to have started with no more than a few men making speeches about their grievances in the canteen. As so often happens, a crowd gathered and cheered the soapbox orators, but apart from a few glasses being smashed the arrival of the shore patrol broke up the meeting and the men returned to their ships. The following evening the shore patrol found very much the same sort of trouble brewing, but this time the doors of the canteen were locked from the inside. The lieutenant in charge forced his way inside and ordered the speechifying to stop, but wisely retreated when he realised that the mood of the crowd had turned ugly. More speeches followed but the reinforced shore patrol succeeded in clearing the canteen and getting the men to return to their ships by 10.00 pm.

Next day the ships were due to start the exercises, but when the battleship *Valiant* tried to go to sea only a few young seamen, senior ratings and marines answered the commands. The battleship *Rodney* also found that no-one would begin the morning's work, and other ships like the *Nelson* and *Hood* were in a similar position. However, it was clear that some ships were unaffected; the *Warspite, Malaya* and *Repulse* went to sea without trouble, and returned later that day to a chorus of booing from the mutinous ships. The cruisers were also less affected, although the *Norfolk* was badly troubled and some of the worst indiscipline occurred in the minelayer *Adventure* (as so often happens, among ratings not affected by the pay-cuts).

Although the 'Invergordon Mutiny' was, like its predecessor at Spithead in 1797, more of a sit-down strike than a bloody uprising of men against their officers, it caused uproar. The Admiralty, having contributed largely to the disaster, made an undignified attempt to pin the blame on the luckless Admiral Tomkinson, who had been hurriedly appointed to relieve the sick C-in-C of the Atlantic Fleet just before the mutiny. The Cabinet saw the hand of Communist agitators behind everything, but above all the reception by the foreign press of the news that the Royal Navy had mutinied (five ships out of only twelve, in point of fact) sent sterling plummeting against other currencies. It had the effect of forcing the British Government to abandon the Gold Standard, a pious wish which had deluded Chancellors of the Exchequer since 1914 – ironically the great economist Maynard Keynes was to point out that going off the Gold Standard was the only way for the British economy to recover from the Slump, so the Invergordon Mutiny was a blessing in disguise.

The Prime Minister Ramsay MacDonald finally acted on 21st September, announcing that cuts were to be limited to 10 per cent, except for higher-ranking officers, and that men on the lowest rates would recive no cut at all. An exhaustive search for Red influence yielded no evidence, but 27 Devonport men were discharged from the Service (the figure was reduced to 24 subsequently), despite a promise of an amnesty by the First Lord, Austen Chamberlain. Other men who had been removed from their ships at Invergordon were posted to the China Station, but without giving their names to the C-in-C, in order to give them a fresh start. A more constructive course might have been to demand the retirement of the Board of Admiralty, for throughout the sad business the men reiterated that they had lost

confidence in the Admiralty, not their officers. But it was still a warning that ultimately officers were responsible for the welfare of their men, and after Invergordon the Navy took care that such a gulf of misunderstanding should not open up again. Indeed the most worrying aspect of the affair was the way in which officers remained sublimely confident until it dawned on them that their ships were not going to sail.

Returning to the dismal story of the search for international disarmament, 1930 had seen the signing of the London Treaty, under which the 'battleship holiday' was extended to 1936 and a complicated formula for the replacement of cruisers was arrived at – it bore heavily on the Royal Navy, which had a greater percentage of ships of all categories which

had seen hard war-service. Japan and the United States were the other signatories, but France and Italy refused to accept any limits on total tonnage. The Germans were still apparently observing the restrictions of the Versailles Treaty, but under protest; they maintained with some justification that they faced a threat from the east, but in fact the *Reichsmarine* at this period never had sufficient manpower to keep all its ships in commission.

The British electors still seemed to believe that nothing would change, and as late as 1933 it was possible for an anti-rearmament candidate to win by a landslide in a local election. When the Oxford Union pompously resolved never to fight for King and Country men like Adolf Hitler and Benito Mussolini could hardly be blamed for thinking that Britain repre-

sented no threat to their ambitions. The United States was hardly in better shape, still making a painful recovery from the Great Depression and staunchly isolationist in sentiment.

Behind the scenes the Admiralty was, however, desperately trying to get funds for replacing the obsolete tonnage and weaponry of the Fleet. What rapidly became evident was that the magnificent performance of British industry in the 1890s and 1900s could not be repeated, for the armaments industry had withered away almost to nothing, starved of funds since the Armistice. To cite one of the

Below: Swordfish torpedo-bombers over the *Ark Royal.* These obsolescent biplanes were to perform remarkable deeds in the war.

worst examples, there was no longer sufficient capacity to produce more than one heavy gun-turret design, and even the combined resources of Vickers-Armstrong (the two companies had amalgamated during the slump) could not guarantee more than two sets of guns before 1940. This lack of production capacity extended right down to destroyer guns and blades for steam turbines, and the Naval Staff realised that they had very few options. No new battleships could be started until 1936, but much worse was a similar prohibition on carriers, and in the meantime the emergence of Hitler as the new leader of Germany was a warning that the breathing-space afforded by the Versailles Treaty had run out. In more ways than one, for the new German Chancellor announced that Germany would shortly begin the construction of U-Boats once more.

There was little choice but to try to slow down German naval expansion by negotiation, and in 1935 the Anglo-German Naval Agreement was signed, limiting the newly renamed *Kriegsmarine* to a total of 35 per cent of the total tonnage of the Royal Navy. To many in Britain it seemed an act of betrayal, or at the very least a meek acceptance of German aggression but posterity has taken a more lenient view. In the absence of any valid international sanctions which could be brought against Germany to enforce the Versailles Treaty's provisions it was better for the Admiralty to get fixed ratios of strength. A hidden advantage to the British was the fact that Hitler *needed* to keep the British friendly until such time as his grand design in Europe was complete. Another helpful provision was the clause which stipulated that any increase in U-Boat tonnage would have to be offset by a reduction in the total for surface warships. The *Kriegsmarine* was still smarting under the disgrace of its mass scuttling at Scapa Flow in 1919, and for prestige reasons as much as political and military, the re-creation of a strong surface fleet was given priority. In any case, a massive expansion of the U-Boat Arm would

merely have alarmed the British, which was against the Führer's express wishes.

In the Mediterranean things seemed better. The Abyssinian Crisis of 1935 provided a much-needed chance to mobilise, and the many weaknesses revealed could be tackled. Sadly the same could not be said for the League of Nations, for its failure to stand firm against Italian aggression marked the last hope of 'collective security' as a means of staving off war, and of course convinced the dictators that they had nothing to fear. On the credit side, the Royal Navy tested its Mobile Naval Base Defence Organisation (MNBDO) with a view to setting up an emergency base at Navarino in Greece; it did not work but it provided the Royal Marines with a foretaste of the Combined Operations role which they would fulfil so successfully in the Second World War. For the first time concerted action with the French Navy was planned; if the British and French had cooperated much earlier the crisis might never have happened, and there seems little doubt that if war had come the two navies would have had little difficulty in handling the Italian Fleet.

Only the Far East remained intractable. The old Anglo-Saxon supremacy was crumbling fast, and the Japanese were in the ascendant. Since Admiral Jellicoe had reported in 1919 that the British should build a fortified naval base at Singapore and station a powerful fleet there, work had actually started on building the base. Despite stops and starts it was well under way by 1936, but the Royal Navy was so badly over-stretched that there could be no question of stationing a fleet at Singapore. Year after year the Dominions, particularly Australia and New Zealand, were assured that in time of war a 'Main Fleet' would be sent to Singapore, and all the Admiralty Board could hope was that Britain would not find herself similarly at war with Germany, Italy and Japan.

The Rearmament Programme began as planned in 1936, but for the reasons already mentioned the results were so meagre that in 1938 during the Munich Crisis the Chiefs of Staff advised the Prime

Minister, Neville Chamberlain, to avoid war at all costs, even if it meant a climb-down over Czechoslovakia. The first of the new battleships and aircraft carriers were in hand, as well as a large number of minor warships, but nothing was ready:

Royal Navy building programme

5 *King George V* Class battleships laid down 1937
2 *Lion* Class battleships to be laid down 1939 (+3 more projected)
4 *Illustrious* Class carriers laid down 1937
2 *Implacable* Class carriers to be laid down 1938-39
2 *Edinburgh* Class cruisers laid down 1936
6 *Dido* Class AA cruisers laid down 1937
4 *Dido* Class to be laid down 1938-39
5 *Fiji* Class cruisers laid down 1938
5 *Fiji* Class to be laid down 1939
10 'Tribal' Class destroyers built 1936-38
6 'Tribal' Class laid down 1936-37
24 *Javelin* Class destroyers laid down 1936-37
16 *Lightning* Class destroyers laid down 1938 (+8 projected)
11 motor torpedo boats ordered 1936-38 (+6 projected)
15 *Triton* Class submarines laid down 1936-37
3 *Unity* Class submarines built 1937-38

The Munich Crisis convinced everybody at last that war was unavoidable, and contingency plans were drawn up for mass-production of various standard types. To remedy the appalling shortage of convoy escorts 20 old destroyers were refitted and 20 new utility destroyers were laid down. A commercial whale-catcher was examined, and the Admiralty decided that it would make the basis of a useful coastal escort – in honour of the useful First World War general-purpose sloops they would become the 'Flower' Class corvettes. The Dominions also re-cognised the common threat and plans were made to build destroyers and corvettes in Australian and Canadian shipyards. In contrast, the Germans were finding great difficulty in coping with their more modest expansion. Under the 1935 Programme they had ordered the battleship *Bismarck*, the carrier *Graf Zeppelin* and the heavy cruiser *Prinz Eugen*; the following year saw the *Tirpitz*, another carrier, the *Peter Strasser* and two heavy cruisers ordered. By 1941 only the two battleships and the *Prinz Eugen* had been completed, and the others had been stopped, whereas during the same period the Royal Navy took delivery of three battleships, three aircraft carriers and 16 cruisers, to say nothing of large numbers of destroyers, submarines and corvettes.

Despite all its tribulations the Royal Navy was still the largest in the world. Its all-volunteer force made it a fighting navy of remarkable calibre, and the disappointments of 1914-18 had done nothing to dim that 'tradition of victory' created in the 17th and 18th centuries.

Above: HMS *Picotee*, one of the new 'Flower' class corvettes, mass-produced to fight the U-Boats.

Below: The old battlecruiser *Renown* was rebuilt to act as a fast carrier escort, just in time for the war.

The cruisers *Glasgow* and *Newcastle* in close formation.

World War II

When war broke out on 3rd September 1939 the British and French governments, so badly equipped in other respects, had one trump card, sea power. The Allies' fundamental strategy differed little from the one they had followed in 1914. The Royal Navy would assume the main burden of preventing the Germans from breaking out into the Atlantic, and the responsibility of bringing war material from the United States and the overseas empire, while the French contained the Italians in the Mediterranean. As for offensive action, both countries were content to build up their strength until such time as a weak spot presented itself.

To achieve these somewhat modest aims the Royal Navy was to follow its traditional policy of dividing its forces into a main battle fleet, the Home Fleet, with battleships and aircraft carriers, while allocating the bulk of its light forces to the protection of trade. This time there was no dispute about the merits of convoying, and right from the outset merchant ships were convoyed around the British Isles and large orders for convoy escorts were placed with British and Canadian shipyards. The Royal Navy had spent a good deal of its scarce resources on the development of a new underwater sensor, known as Asdic (but now known as Sonar), and in addition to fitting 200 destroyers had plans for equipping trawlers, corvettes and sloops with the device.

The first round nevertheless went to the U-Boats, when two weeks after the outbreak of war the carrier HMS *Courageous* was torpedoed in the Western

Right: The First Sea Lord, Admiral Sir Dudley Pound (right) talks to Admiral King, the US Navy's Commander in Chief.

Below: French and British warships lying at Alexandria, early in 1940.

Approaches. Three days earlier the new carrier *Ark Royal* had been narrowly missed by a spread of torpedoes from *U.39*, and it was realised that these ships were too valuable to be risked on aimless patrolling in submarine-infested waters. Even more discouraging was the sinking of the battleship *Royal Oak* in Scapa Flow on 8th October. The old ship, a veteran of Jutland, was no longer a front-line unit of the battle fleet but the news that *U.47* had been able to penetrate the Home Fleet's main base came as an unpleasant shock. There was talk of sabotage but the facts speak for themselves; the line of blockships sunk in 1915 had worked about during 24 years of winter gales, leaving sufficient water at high tide for Kapitän-

leutnant Günther Prien to take *U.47* into the Flow and out again.

In the months to come the Home Fleet had to be dispersed to bases on the west coast of Scotland, in much the same way as the Grand Fleet had been forced to leave its main base at the end of 1914. The battleships *Nelson* and *Barham* were both damaged, one by a magnetic mine and the other by a torpedo, but this did not stop the Home Fleet from escorting three large convoys of troopships from Canada. On more than one occasion the German battlecruisers *Scharnhorst* and *Gneisenau* tried to get to grips with a convoy but they were always deterred by the sight of the tripod mast of a First World War veteran battleship – Hitler's admirals were

no more willing to risk damage to their ships than the Kaiser's before them, and they missed priceless opportunities to cut the Atlantic lifeline.

At the end of the year came the heartening news of the Battle of the River Plate, when the 'pocket battleship' *Admiral Graf Spee* was run to earth off the coast of Uruguay. She was a large armoured cruiser designed as a commerce-raider, and although somewhat overrated by the British press her six 11-inch guns and 4-inch armour made her a formidable opponent for any cruiser. Fortunately she was trapped by three cruisers, the small 6-inch-gunned *Ajax* and *Achilles* (the latter manned by the Royal New Zealand Navy) and the 8-inch-gunned heavy

Above: Survivors clinging to the shattered hull of the destroyer *Glowworm*, seen through a rangefinder aboard the *Admiral Hipper*.

Left: The destroyer *Grafton* on her way to evacuate troops from Dunkirk.

cruiser *Exeter*. Commodore Harwood followed a drill which had been worked out before the war, keeping his ships widely dispersed and using their 6-knot advantage in speed to stay out of trouble.

As always the German fire was accurate, but even though the *Graf Spee* put all three of HMS *Exeter*'s turrets out of action and two in HMS *Ajax* the cruisers could still steam, and the threat of a torpedo-attack forced Captain Langsdorff to keep his distance. The constant picador tactics of the small cruisers saved the *Exeter* and finally the pocket battleship broke off the action and headed for neutral Uruguayan waters to repair her damage. There she was subjected to intense diplomatic pressure as the British tried to persuade the Uruguayan authorities not to intern her. There was also a war of nerves, with false rumours suggesting that the carrier *Ark*

Royal and the battlecruiser *Renown* were nearby. Finally it was Hitler's nerve which broke, and he ordered Langsdorff to scuttle the *Graf Spee* rather than risk her capture or internment.

What the press chose to call the 'Phoney War' came to an end in April 1940, when German forces invaded Denmark and Norway. In fact the First Lord of the Admiralty, Winston Churchill, had been urging an operation to cut off the iron ore traffic from the northern Norwegian port of Narvik to Germany, and at about the same time that German naval forces got under way for Norway the British moved a force of mine-laying destroyers into the Inner Leads. Everybody was taken by surprise, including the British, even though a Polish submarine had already reported torpedoing a German troopship which was on the way to Bergen. Only at Oslo did the Germans meet any setback, when a party of stout-hearted coastal gunners sank the new heavy cruiser *Blücher*, but after the light cruiser *Königsberg* was damaged at Bergen a force of Fleet Air Arm dive-bombers arrived from the Orkneys and sank her at her moorings.

British forces were ordered to intervene, and on 9th April HMS *Renown* fought an indecisive action with the *Scharnhorst* and *Gneisenau*. A day later Captain Warburton-Lee took five destroyers up Narvik Fjord to destroy the six German destroyers believed to be there. There were in fact 10 enemy destroyers, but this did not deter the 2nd Destroyer Flotilla, which succeeded in sinking two destroyers and damaging five more before numbers began to tell. Warburton-Lee was killed and the *Hardy* and *Hunter* were lost, but on their way down the fjord the survivors sank the transport bringing spare ammunition, sealing the fate of Commodore Bonte's flotilla.

Three days later Admiral Whitworth took his flagship the battleship *Warspite* and nine destroyers into Narvik Fjord to finish the work started by Warburton-Lee. This time it was a rout, with 15-inch salvoes booming down the fjord, while the battleship's floatplane spotted all the hiding places of the German destroyers. Not a single destroyer escaped, nor a U-Boat hiding there, and the only casualty was a British destroyer which had her bow blown off by a torpedo.

Heartening though the two Battles of Narvik might be, they did nothing to regain control of Norway, and soon the hastily assembled Anglo-French expeditionary force had to be evacuated. In the long run, however, the Allies inflicted grievous losses on the German Navy which it could not afford. On 20th June the *Gneisenau* was put out of action by a torpedo from a submarine, and her sister *Scharnhorst* was similarly damaged by a destroyer while sinking the carrier *Glorious*.

Suddenly the war took a disastrous turn. On 10th May 1940 the German Army smashed through the flimsy defences of Belgium and northern France, and within a fortnight had destroyed the British and French armies. Apart from pockets of resistance, all that was left was an Anglo-French perimeter around the port of Dunkirk, and the people of Britain awoke to the first real threat of invasion since the days of Napoleon's Army of England. The Dutch Army surrendered, and then a British destroyer took Queen Wilhelmina and her family to safety, and the French Navy succeeded in blocking Antwerp, Zeebrugge and Ostend.

On 19th May the Admiralty received a request from the War Cabinet for advice on the chances of getting the survivors of the British Expeditionary Force out of France. Next day the Flag Officer, Dover, Admiral Ramsay started detailed planning for Operation 'Dynamo', and by the time it was finished a total of 400,000 men had been brought home. Although often described as a miracle it was miraculous planning rather than a series of accidents. The famous 'little ships' were brought in deliberately, to speed the transfer of soldiers from open beaches to the destroyers and personnel ships, and at the same time 2000 tons of ammunition were taken in each day to supply the rearguard. Miracle or not, the figures are still hard to believe: by 4th June 338,226 men had been brought out of Dunkirk, at a cost of 72 ships of all kinds sunk, 163 lost in collisions and 45 damaged. Operations 'Aerial' and 'Cycle' then lifted another 191,000 men from the Biscay ports between 16th

Far right: HMS *Sheffield* lying at Gibraltar in August 1940.

Below: HMS *Havant*, recently taken over from Brazil, was sunk at Dunkirk.

and 26th June, and it proved possible to tow a number of French warships away from the dockyards. Hitler's army and air force had scored a magnificent tactical victory, but they had failed strategically by not crippling the British, who could once again withdraw behind their moat to lick their wounds and rebuild.

What was to become known as the Battle of the Atlantic now began in earnest, for what the British had always feared was now reality; the Germans had reached the Channel ports and could strike at the Atlantic with impunity. But for the moment the Battle of Britain occupied both British and German planners. The British Expeditionary Force had left behind all its artillery and tanks, and in theory at least, it was in no shape to resist a German invasion. As early as 21st May 1940 Grand-Admiral Raeder had put forward a tentative proposal, but the first directive from Hitler did not appear until 16th July, when he announced Operation 'Sealion'. In just one month the German Army Staff prepared a plan for a broad-front landing between Ramsgate and the Isle of Wight, only to discover that their Navy colleagues were aghast at its deficiencies.

The *Ark Royal* launches a Swordfish torpedo-bomber.

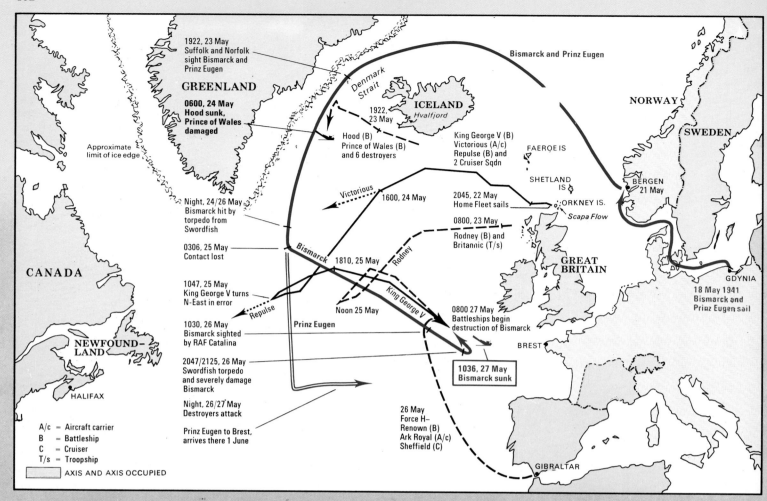

1922, 23 May
Suffolk and Norfolk
sight Bismarck and
Prinz Eugen

Bismarck and Prinz Eugen

GREENLAND

Denmark Strait

ICELAND
Hvalfjord

NORWAY

**0600, 24 May
Hood sunk,
Prince of Wales
damaged**

1922,
23 May

Hood (B)
Prince of Wales (B)
and 6 destroyers

King George V (B)
Victorious (A/c)
Repulse (B) and
2 Cruiser Sqdn

SWEDEN

FAERØE IS

Approximate
limit of ice edge

SHETLAND
IS

Victorious

1600, 24 May

2045, 22 May
Home Fleet sails

BERGEN
21 May

Night, 24/26 May
Bismarck hit by
torpedo from
Swordfish

ORKNEY IS.
Scapa Flow

0800, 23 May
Rodney (B) and
Britannic (T/s)

CANADA

Bismarck

0306, 25 May
Contact lost

1810, 25 May

Rodney

**GREAT
BRITAIN**

GDYNIA

1047, 25 May
King George V turns
N-East in error

King George V

Repulse

Noon 25 May

0800 27 May
Battleships begin
destruction of Bismarck

18 May 1941
Bismarck and
Prinz Eugen sail

**NEWFOUND-
LAND**

Prinz Eugen

BREST

1030, 26 May
Bismarck sighted
by RAF Catalina

**1036, 27 May
Bismarck sunk**

2047/2125, 26 May
Swordfish torpedo
and severely damage
Bismarck

HALIFAX

Night, 26/27 May
Destroyers attack

26 May
Force H–
Renown (B)
Ark Royal (A/c)
Sheffield (C)

Prinz Eugen to Brest,
arrives there 1 June

A/c = Aircraft carrier
B = Battleship
C = Cruiser
T/s = Troopship

GIBRALTAR

AXIS AND AXIS OCCUPIED

Top left: The cruiser *Trinidad* (right) refuels a destroyer in the Arctic in 1942.

Top right: Vice Admiral Sir Bruce Fraser, who succeeded Sir John Tovey as Commander-in-Chief of the Home Fleet.

Below: HMS *Musketeer* and her sisters of the 'M' class were modified for Arctic service, with asbestos insulation and steam heating for guns and torpedo tubes.

Above: The old destroyer *Vivacious* alongside the Dunkirk Mole. In the foreground is a sunken trawler.

'Sealion' was taken very seriously by the British in 1940 and even today it is fashionable to talk as if Britain was only spared from invasion because Hitler lost interest in the scheme. This is far too simple a view of what went wrong. The most obvious setback was the Luftwaffe's failure to subdue the Royal Air Force, but the failure to take account of British sea power was even more important. The German Navy, having lost a major part of its strength in Norway, could not hope to oppose the large number of ships which the Royal Navy kept in home waters. Another problem was the total ignorance of amphibious warfare techniques shown by the generals; as the navy staff officers complained, the soldiers seemed to think that they were crossing a river, rather than one of the most treacherous stretches of water in northern Europe.

Every night the RAF raided the invasion ports, while British warships shelled the tightly packed Rhine barges from seaward. In 1803 Lord St Vincent had told Parliament, 'I do not say the French cannot come, only that they cannot come by sea.' In October 1940 another distinguished sailor, Sir Charles Forbes, the Commander in Chief of the Home Fleet, tried to still his countrymen's fears. He told Winston Churchill that while the British remained predominant at sea, and until Germany had defeated RAF Fighter Command, invasion by sea was not a practical operation of war. He pointed out that it was quite

easy to spot the likeliest targets of the German invasion:
1. They would certainly be within range of shore-based aircraft.
2. An invasion could not be supplied through the winter without capturing a port, all of which were heavily defended.
3. A sudden raid under cover of fog was unlikely, since there were on average only five foggy days per month.

What Forbes was asking was that anti-invasion precautions should not take precedence over normal naval defence of trade, but he was not believed until it was learned in 1941 that Hitler had finally cancelled 'Sealion' in favour of the attack on Russia. The great English adventure was deferred on 17th September, again on 12th October, and finally 'held over for reconsideration' until 1941.

The Battle of the Atlantic – 1940-41

As in 1915 and 1917, the failure of other means of attack led the German Navy inevitably to an all-out attack on British trade, and from the summer of 1940 the Battle of the Atlantic began in earnest. Up to the end of May 1940 the Royal Navy's Western Approaches Command had only been escorting convoys 200 miles west of Ireland, but between July and October the limit was extended to 19° West. From its dispersal point the convoy then sailed in company for another 24 hours before proceeding independently while the escorts picked up an incoming convoy. On the other side of the Atlantic the Royal Canadian Navy's Halifax Escort Force provided a similar local escort, but in be-

tween these two forces the ships could normally rely on only one escort, usually an armed merchant cruiser.

New corvettes and destroyers were beginning to come forward in numbers, but by September 1940 the total of British destroyers had actually fallen from 184 to 171, with only 21 new ships replacing the 34 sunk, and nearly half of those 171 were under refit or repair. To remedy this desperate shortage of destroyers Winston Churchill asked President Roosevelt to lend 50 elderly destroyers from the US Navy's 'mothball fleet', in exchange for base rights in the Caribbean and the Atlantic. The deal went through, and to commemorate their American ancestry the ships were given names of towns common to the USA and the British Commonwealth. In spite of their age the ships gave exceptional service until 1944 and their arrival in the North Atlantic made all the difference between victory and defeat.

In October 1940 Admiral Dönitz introduced the 'wolf pack' technique or *rudeltaktik*, basically an attempt to swamp a convoy's defences by attacking from all directions under cover of darkness. By December 1940 the total of shipping sunk had climbed to 2,186,000 tons, having reached a peak for one month of 352,400 tons in October. In 1941 the figures started to climb again, and by May they had topped 325,000 tons. In October that year there were 80 operational U-Boats, as against 22 in January, with only 21 lost.

To answer this terrible onslaught the British had to muster their best scientific brains. Radar had been in its infancy at the

outbreak of the war; although experimental sets had been sent to sea as early as 1936 the first set capable of detecting a U-Boat on the surface (Type 271) did not get to sea in a corvette until May 1941. Almost as important as radar was high-frequency direction-finding (nicknamed huff-duff) which could give accurate 'fixes' on U-Boats transmitting the course and position of a convoy. Huff-duff provided escorts with the whereabouts of individual U-Boats, while the Admiralty had the even bigger advantage that they could read the operational orders sent by Admiral Dönitz. Polish intelligence officers had provided the British with a German Enigma ciphering machine in 1939, and this head start gave the Director of Naval Intelligence the chance to break into the German naval ciphers. All information gleaned in this way was carefully handled to protect the source, and only senior officers were allowed to read signals marked 'Ultra.'

Aircraft proved a great help in protecting convoys, but the difficulty lay in getting them to accompany a convoy all the way across the Atlantic. Air bases in Iceland helped but in 1941 there was still no aircraft capable of covering the 'Black Gap' in the middle of the North Atlantic. A few merchant ships were fitted with a catapult on the forecastle, to enable them to launch fighters to shoot down long-range reconnaissance aircraft, but the real solution was to provide small carriers. In August 1941 the first 'escort carrier' HMS *Audacity* appeared, an ex-German banana boat fitted with a wooden flight deck on which were parked six Martlet

fighter aircraft. The *Audacity* lasted only three months before being torpedoed but she had proved the point, and further escort carriers were ordered from American shipyards.

The Mediterranean – 1940-41
In the Mediterranean things had gone well at first. A short action had disabled the French Fleet at Mers-el-Kebir, forestalling any Italian or German move to take it over by treachery, and within a week the Mediterranean Fleet met the Italians in the

Above: The *Renown, Illustrious, Valiant* and *Ark Royal* in the Mediterranean in 1940.

Battle of Calabria. Although the enemy disappeared over the horizon at high speed the flagship *Warspite* was able to land a 15-inch shell on the *Giulio Cesare* at the stupendous range of 15 miles (still a record for hitting a ship under way). The moral ascendancy over the Italians was

Below: A 'chariot' human torpedo, copied from the Italian *Maiale*.

confirmed 11 days later when HMAS *Sydney* sank the light cruiser *Bartolomeo Colleoni* off Crete. In August 1940 the first of the new carriers, HMS *Illustrious*, arrived with other reinforcements, and the C-in-C Admiral Andrew Cunningham was able to begin a dazzling run of successes. On the night of 11th November he sent in 21 Swordfish torpedo-bombers to attack the main Italian base at Taranto, and at a cost of only two aircraft the battleship *Conte di Cavour* was sunk, two more battleships were damaged and the seaplane base was wrecked.

Taranto was a notable 'first' for naval aviation, and its implications were not lost on the Japanese, but for the Fleet Air Arm it was a vindication – in two hours they had accomplished more than the entire Grand Fleet had at Jutland and at considerably less cost in lives.

So great a threat to enemy communications was the carrier *Illustrious* that the German Air Force sent a specially trained Stuka formation to the Mediterranean to sink her. They failed to do so, but only

Above: The 6-inch guns of the cruiser *Mauritius* firing in support of the 5th Army in Sicily, 1943.

Below: Two of Lord Louis Mountbatten's famous 5th Flotilla, HMS *Kipling* (foreground) and *Kimberley*.

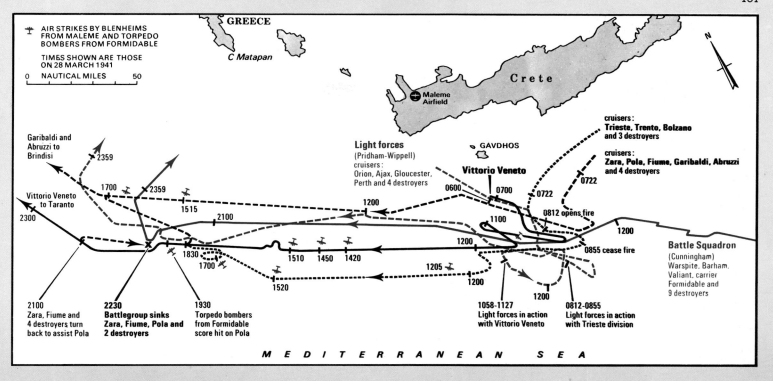

AIR STRIKES BY BLENHEIMS
FROM MALEME AND TORPEDO
BOMBERS FROM FORMIDABLE

TIMES SHOWN ARE THOSE
ON 28 MARCH 1941

0   NAUTICAL MILES   50

GREECE

C Matapan

Crete

Maleme
Airfield

GAVDHOS

N

cruisers:
Trieste, Trento, Bolzano
and 3 destroyers

cruisers:
Zara, Pola, Fiume, Garibaldi, Abruzzi
and 4 destroyers

Light forces
(Pridham-Wippell)
cruisers:
Orion, Ajax, Gloucester,
Perth and 4 destroyers

Vittorio Veneto

Garibaldi and
Abruzzi to
Brindisi

2359

1700   2359

1515

2100

Vittorio Veneto
to Taranto

2300

0600   0700   0722   0722

0812 opens fire

1200

1100

1200

1830

1700   1510   1450   1420

1520   1205

1200

0855 cease fire

1200

1200

1200

2100
Zara, Fiume and
4 destroyers turn
back to assist Pola

2230
Battlegroup sinks
Zara, Fiume, Pola and
2 destroyers

1930
Torpedo bombers
from Formidable
score hit on Pola

1058-1127
Light forces in action
with Vittorio Veneto

0812-0855
Light forces in action
with Trieste division

Battle Squadron
(Cunningham)
Warspite, Barham,
Valiant, carrier
Formidable and
9 destroyers

M E D I T E R R A N E A N   S E A

because her armoured flight deck and rugged construction saved her, and she had to go to the United States for massive repairs in January 1941, leaving the Mediterranean without a modern carrier. In spite of this Cunningham sought out the Italians once more, and in March 1941, as soon as the new carrier HMS *Formidable* arrived he took the offensive. A torpedo-bomber slowed down the Italian battleship *Vittorio Veneto*, and while Cunningham's battleships were searching for her that night they ran into three heavy cruisers. In a short, one-sided action the *Warspite, Valiant* and *Barham* sank the *Fiume, Pola* and *Zara* without suffering damage themselves. The Battle of Matapan was proof that the Navy had exorcised the ghost of Jutland, for the night-fighting drill, gunnery and communications had all worked superbly.

Such was the success of the British, both on land and sea, that the Germans were forced to come to the rescue of their Italian allies. In April 1941 Greece was overrun swiftly, and a rash British attempt to send troops was thrown headlong into reverse. No sooner had the survivors reached Crete than they were under attack again, and the Navy was ordered to get them out. Losses were savage as the Mediterranean Fleet took the brunt of air attack without air cover, and nearly all the major units of the Fleet were hit. Cunningham was urged to leave the Army to its fate, as the losses had reached an unbearable level, but as he put it so succinctly, 'It takes three years to build a ship, and 300 years to build a tradition.' The Fleet stayed, and somehow the bulk of the defenders of Crete were got back to

Above: The sky fills with flak bursts as the Operation 'Pedestal' convoy battles through to Malta in August 1942.

Far right: HMS *Rodney* and an escorting AA cruiser off the North African coast.

Bottom right: Operation 'Husky' was a large amphibious landing in Sicily, necessary to secure the Central Meditarranean.

Alexandria. It might not have succeeded had the Italian Navy come out of harbour.

The British had become over-confident, and now they faced a long period of adversity, in which the island fortress of Malta would come close to being starved into submission and the last capital units would be at the bottom of the sea or out of action in Alexandria. The *Ark Royal* was finally sunk in November 1941, followed by the battleship *Barham*, and the following month Italian 'human torpedoes' put Cunningham's last two battleships, the *Queen Elizabeth* and *Valiant* out of action, but still the Royal Navy did not lose control of the Mediterranean.

The Atlantic – May 1941 to May 1943

The pre-war planning of the German Navy had envisaged a two-pronged attack on British trade. Capital ships and cruisers were to operate on the high seas, attacking convoys and driving off or sinking their escorts, and then the U-Boats would have a free hand to slaughter the unprotected merchant ships. The 32,000-ton battlecruisers *Scharnhorst* and *Gneisenau* had tried this without much success in 1940, but in 1941 the new 41,000-ton battleship *Bismarck* was ready and as she was the equal of any ship in the Royal Navy the *Kriegsmarine* planned a

160

Left: A Catapult-Armed Merchantman (CAM-Ship), one of the expedients adopted to protect convoys from air attack.

old, had never had her magazine protection modernised, and was hit at a range at which the German 15-inch guns would have the best chance of penetrating her thin deck-armour. Had she been able to close the range by another 3000-4000 yards she would have become progressively less vulnerable, and the outcome might have been very different. As it was, the pride of the Royal Navy and 1416 officers and men had been wiped out.

For three days every ship and aircraft which could be spared was thrown into the hunt, and ships converged on the South-Western Approaches. The *Bismarck* was known to be heading for Brest, where she could join the two German battlecruisers and continue to menace the Atlantic convoys, so it was imperative to sink her before she got within range of shore-based air cover. The carrier *Victorious* carried out one unsuccessful torpedo-strike but on 26th May the *Ark Royal*'s Swordfish succeeded in knocking out the *Bismarck*'s rudders and reducing her speed to 5 knots.

At first light next morning the battleships *Rodney* and *King George V* hove in sight, and opened fire at 16,000 yards. Half an hour later the *Bismarck* was silenced and the *Rodney* had closed to 4000 yards, vainly trying to sink the battered wreck, which was now too low in the water for the British salvoes to penetrate her armoured deck. Finally the heavy cruiser *Dorsetshire* closed in and sank the tortured hulk of the *Bismarck* with a salvo of torpedoes. Thus ended the last attempt to use the German Fleet on the high seas, for the *Tirpitz* was to spend her days moored in Norwegian fjords and the cherished idea of a joint foray by the *Scharnhorst* and *Gneisenau* was replaced by orders to get the two battlecruisers back to German waters.

The sands were running out for the Thousand-Year Reich, for the United States of America was now closely involved in supporting Britain, and it was only a matter of time before she joined the war. The Lend-Lease Act in March 1941 started to give the Royal Navy the extra warships it so desperately needed, and by August 1941 US warships were escorting American merchant ships in a so-called Defence Zone. In October 1941 a U-Boat damaged the destroyer USS *Kearney*, a sign that hostilities could not be avoided much longer, but even when the *Reuben James* was sunk two weeks later the strength of isolationism was still too much for President Roosevelt to declare war on Nazi Germany. Only the hare-brained

further foray into the Atlantic, in company with the heavy cruiser *Prinz Eugen*.

At first the operation was a brilliant success, for the two ships slipped into the North Atlantic without being seen, but in the Denmark Strait between Iceland and Greenland they were spotted on radar by the heavy cruisers *Norfolk* and *Suffolk*. On 23rd May the new battleship *Prince of Wales* and the battlecruiser *Hood* intercepted the two German ships and hastened to bring them to action. Sadly

after only eight minutes' firing the flagship *Hood* caught fire and blew up, in a manner all too reminiscent of her predecessors at Jutland 25 years earlier. The *Prince of Wales* fought back bravely, and even scored two hits on the *Bismarck*, but there could be no question of a brand-new, not yet fully-efficient, ship taking on the *Bismarck* single-handed, and she was ordered to break off the action.

The exact reason for the *Hood*'s loss will never be known, but she was 21 years

Left: HMS *Clare*, one of the 50 destroyers lent by the US Navy in 1940. She had two boilers replaced by extra fuel.

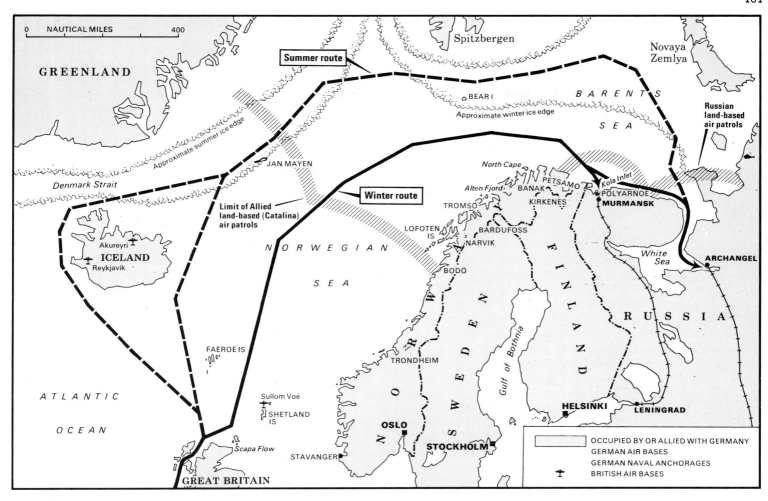

declaration of war by Adolf Hitler, hard on the heels of the Japanese attack on Pearl Harbor, was sufficient to bring the United States into the war against Germany.

Instead of lightening the burden in the Battle of the Atlantic the entry of America into the war merely provided the U-Boats with more targets, and for the first six months shipping losses off the US East Coast were enormous, until emergency anti-submarine measures could be instituted. The Allies now had the additional burden of supplying war material to Russia, and convoys of scarce shipping had to run the gauntlet of German air bases and the U-Boats, all the way to Murmansk and back. To avoid the summer nights of almost perpetual daylight the Russian convoys had to sail during the winter months, when the weather was as bad an enemy as the Germans. Some of the worst convoy actions of all were fought on the 'Kola Run', such as PQ-17, in which 24 out of 37 merchant ships were sunk as a result of a premature order to the convoy to scatter.

The climax of the war against the U-Boats came in March 1943. The shipping losses were now at such a level that both President Roosevelt and Prime Minister Churchill knew that it was simply a question of whether American and Canadian

shipyards could build ships faster than they were being sunk. A series of ferocious convoy battles in March threatened to shatter the whole convoy system, for the Admiralty came close to abandoning it as a countermeasure. When 40 U-Boats attacked convoys SC.122 and HX.229 the two convoys combined, but the U-Boats still sank 21 ships totalling 141,000 tons. But salvation was close at hand, for a number of fresh escort groups, including some of the new escort carriers, which

had been withdrawn to cover the amphibious landings in North Africa at the end of 1942, were now back in the North Atlantic. There were also a number of long-range aircraft such as the VLR (Very Long Range) Liberator bombers, flying from Iceland and the Azores. It was also a period when Allied scientists gained the upper hand over their German counterparts, and a new centimetric wavelength radar set was now being used by anti-submarine aircraft.

Right: HMS *Tartar*, one of the famous 'Tribal' class destroyers.

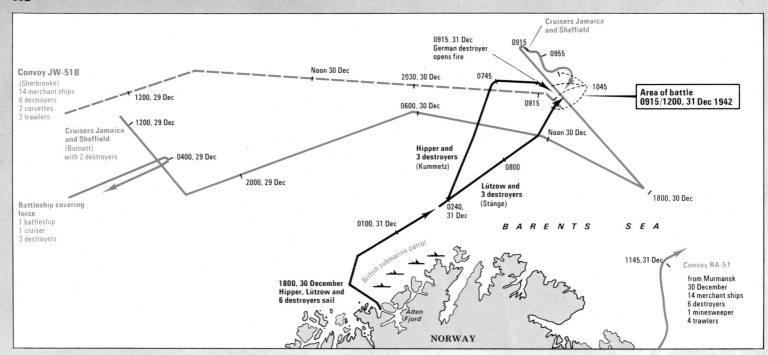

Convoy JW-51B
(Sherbrooke)
14 merchant ships
6 destroyers
2 corvettes
2 trawlers

Cruisers Jamaica
and Sheffield
(Burnett)
with 2 destroyers

Battleship covering
force
1 battleship
1 cruiser
3 destroyers

1200, 29 Dec

1200, 29 Dec

0400, 29 Dec

2000, 29 Dec

Noon 30 Dec

2030, 30 Dec

0600, 30 Dec

0745

0915

0915, 31 Dec
German destroyer
opens fire

Cruisers Jamaica
and Sheffield

0915

0955

1045

**Area of battle
0915/1200, 31 Dec 1942**

Noon 30 Dec

1800, 30 Dec

Hipper and
3 destroyers
(Kummetz)

Lützow and
3 destroyers
(Stänge)

0800

0240,
31 Dec

0100, 31 Dec

British submarine patrol

1800, 30 December
Hipper, Lützow and
6 destroyers sail

Alten
Fjord

NORWAY

B A R E N T S   S E A

1145, 31 Dec

Convoy RA-51

from Murmansk
30 December
14 merchant ships
6 destroyers
1 minesweeper
4 trawlers

Right: The ex-American destroyer HMS
Ludlow.

Below: The corvette *Clematis* going to the
rescue of a coaster.

As had happened in 1917, the reversal of fortunes was rapid. In the second half of March 1943 the scale of U-Boat attacks slackened perceptibly, and in April the losses of merchant ships fell by half. In April 15 U-Boats were sunk, but in May the figure jumped to 41, and by 22nd May Dönitz had to admit defeat and withdrew his battered U-Boats for regrouping. Although they were to return to the fray a few months later the tide had turned against them, and they never represented such a threat to the Allies again. By September 1943 the massive output of new ships had overhauled the tonnage sunk, and it was time to think of taking the offensive.

Although the weather remained a constant foe the Arctic convoys began to find some improvement as the pendulum swung in the Allies' favour. In December 1942 eight Royal Navy destroyers fought the epic Battle of the Barents Sea against the pocket battleship *Lutzow* and the heavy cruiser *Admiral Hipper*, forcing them to give up their attack on the convoy, and delaying them until the arrival of the cruisers *Jamaica* and *Sheffield*. When Hitler heard of this miserable performance he ranted against the cowardice and incompetence of the *Kriegsmarine* in such violent terms that his naval C-in-C Admiral Raeder resigned. Although Hitler later withdrew his threat to scrap all the surface warships, the appointment of Karl Dönitz to command the Navy marked the final acceptance that the main effort must go to the U-Boat Arm.

There was to be one more foray by the surface fleet, however, for Admiral Dönitz knew that the threat of a major surface attack was the only thing which could force a convoy to scatter. On 26th December 1943 the *Scharnhorst* tried to intercept a convoy bound for Murmansk. After being held off by the cruisers *Norfolk, Sheffield* and *Belfast* she returned to the attack later that day, only to discover that the battleship *Duke of York* had now caught up with the convoy. The *Scharnhorst* was battered by accurate salvoes of 14-inch shells, and when she attempted to get clear British and Norwegian destroyers slowed her down with torpedo-hits. The *Duke of York* caught up once more, firing on radar bearings into the Arctic night and when the cruiser *Jamaica* turned into the smoke to fire torpedoes there was no sign of the *Scharnhorst*, apart from 200 shocked survivors.

The war in Europe was to last another 18 months and many more ships were to be sunk, but the German Navy never regained the initiative. The morale of U-Boat personnel remained high to the end, but they could no longer hope to do more than delay the final outcome. The *Kriegsmarine* could do nothing to stop the Allied amphibious landings in Normandy in June 1944, in which no fewer than 7 battleships, 23 cruisers and 105 destroyers took part, to say nothing of thousands of escorts, landing craft and transports. There is no space to describe the naval operations during the Normandy landings, but they marked the height of the Royal Navy's effort in the whole war. Without those cruel losses in the Mediterranean and the Arctic D-Day would not have been possible.

Although the public revered the 'Mighty 'Ood' as the world's largest capital ship she was in fact poorly protected against long-range shellfire.

Left: Casualties being helped aboard the cruiser *Frobisher* on D-Day.

Below: A small part of the gigantic armada of transports and warships off the Normandy beaches on D-Day, 6 June, 1944.

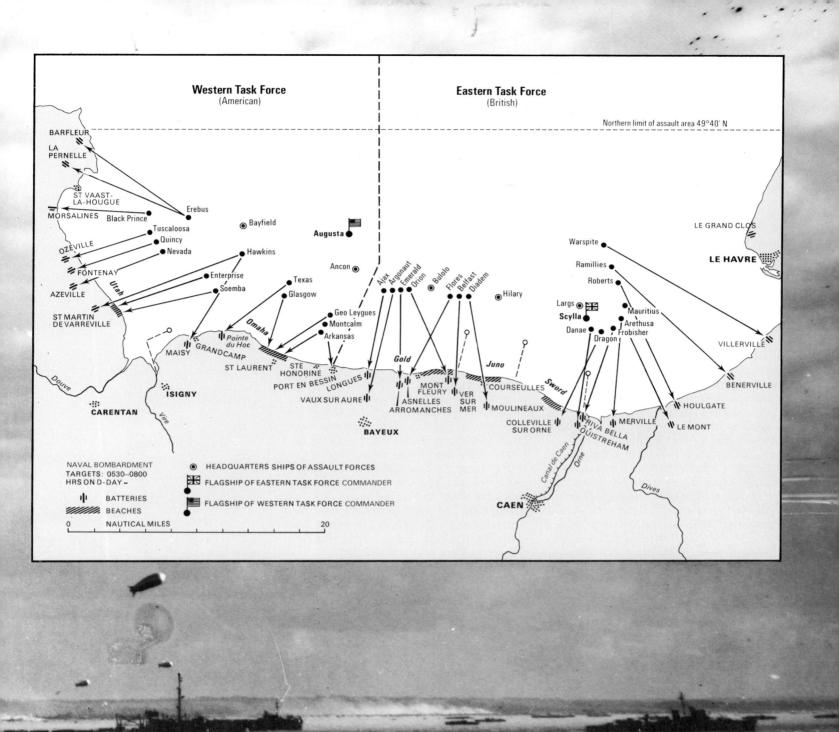

The Far East

The British position in the Far East at the end of 1941 was precarious. Despite all the portents of Japanese intentions no joint plan was drawn up with the US Navy until just before Pearl Harbor. After all the plans to send a main fleet to Singapore all that could be spared were the battleship *Prince of Wales* and the battlecruiser *Repulse*, in a vain attempt to overawe the Japanese. The destruction of the US Pacific Fleet on 7th December robbed that plan of whatever dubious validity it might have enjoyed, and on the 10th the two ships were sunk off the coast of Malaya by a force of torpedo-bombers. The 'Gibraltar of the Far East' turned out to be a paper tiger, and Singapore lasted only three months before it fell to an inferior force of Japanese.

The double debacle left the East Indies wide open, and Japanese air and naval forces rampaged down the island chain, heading for New Guinea and Australia. A combined force of American, British, Dutch and Australian (ABDA) ships did their best to stem the tide but they were overwhelmed. Their last battle in the Java Sea in February 1942 was a gallant but futile act of defiance, and it seemed that nothing could prevent the Japanese from overrunning the entire Western Pacific.

As we know the US Navy was able to match the Japanese, at first in a limited way at the Battle of the Coral Sea in May 1942 and then at Midway the following month, but the Royal Navy had no part in these victories. All that could be done was to send the carrier *Victorious* to the Pacific in 1943, where she operated with the US Navy to alleviate the serious shortage of American carriers at that time. Very

little could be done to get ships out to the Pacific, although the Royal Australian and Royal New Zealand Navies fought alongside the US Navy in many battles. Not until 1944 were there sufficient ships to spare to form a British Pacific Fleet. By March 1944 three carriers and three capital ships were in the East Indies, and on 19 April the British carriers and the USS *Saratoga* launched a devastating air strike on Sabang in North West Sumatra.

The full British Pacific Fleet played a part in the attack on the Ryukyu Islands early in 1945. The four modern battleships bombarded land targets and the armoured carriers proved that they could stand up to *kamikaze* attacks. All of them were hit but none of them was forced to withdraw from the battle. In the East Indies a small force of five destroyers fought the Royal Navy's last classic destroyer action, when they sank the heavy cruiser *Haguro*.

By comparison with the might of the US Navy the British Pacific Fleet might rank as no more than a task force but its presence in Tokyo on the day of the Japanese surrender was a reminder that in its way the Royal Navy had done what it could to bring about the downfall of Japan. It had much to learn from the Americans in carrier operation and refuelling at sea, to name only two examples, but the performance of the British carriers at Okinawa showed that in some respects the Royal Navy was still unique.

Right: The Australian destroyer HMAS *Nepal* receiving a line from the battleship *Queen Elizabeth* in the Indian Ocean, 1944.

Below: An Albacore torpedo-bomber taking off from the carrier *Victorious*.

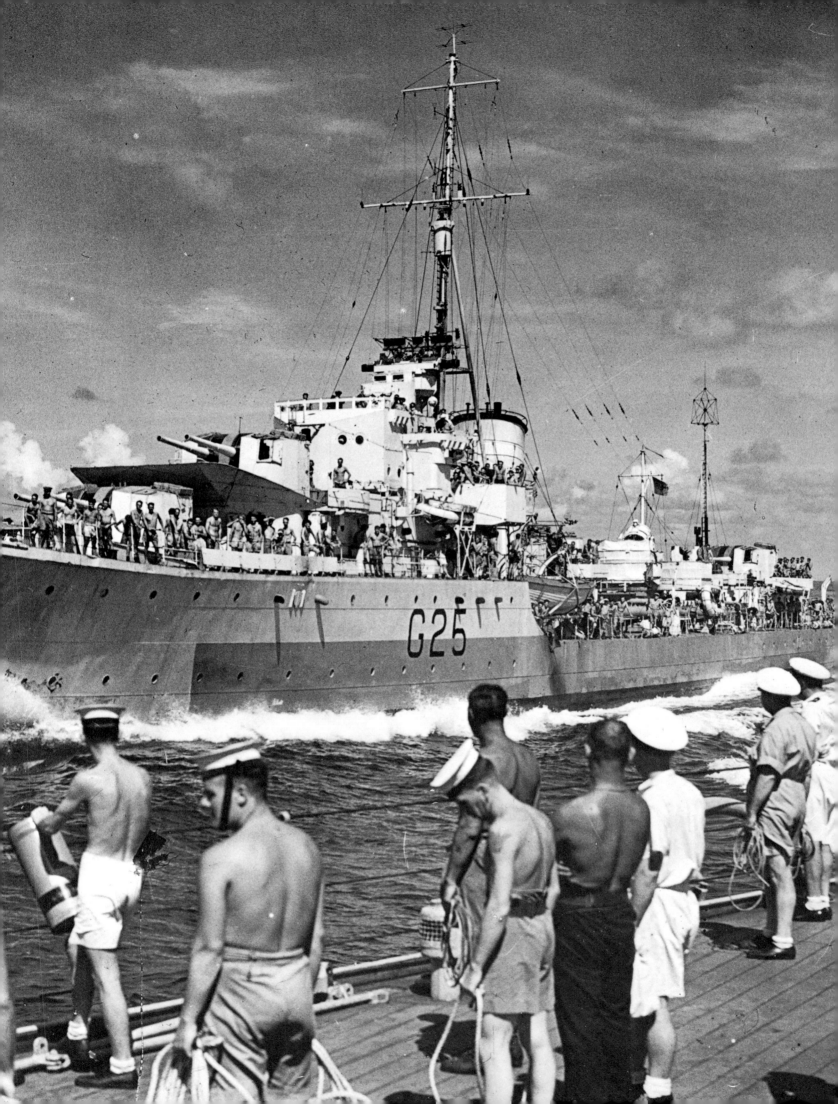

The last British fleet carrier, HMS *Ark Royal* was completed in 1955 and served until 1978.

From Cuts to San Carlos Water

When the Second World War ended in August 1945 the Royal Navy stood at an all-time high: 8940 ships of all sizes, 790,000 officers and men, 74,000 Wrens, and 1336 front-line aircraft. There were also some 4500 merchantmen and 1200 fishing craft, as well as 450 foreign-owned ships, all of which had to be returned to their original owners as soon as possible. As always the rundown was rapid, and by the end of 1946 some 840 warships had been struck off the Navy List and contracts for more than 700 new warships had been cancelled. Beating swords into ploughshares was the order of the day, and shipyards had to concentrate on rebuilding the Merchant Navy as a matter of urgency.

It was a different world from the one which the Royal Navy had known in 1939. From uneasy parity the US Navy had now mushroomed into an enormous fleet, whereas Britain's industrial base had shrunk to a fraction of its pre-war strength, and although successive Admiralty Boards were to fight to maintain an effective Navy the money was no longer there. Not that the threat had abated, for as Winston Churchill put it, an Iron Curtain was descending on Eastern Europe, and Western leaders reluctantly came to accept that the world had exchanged Hitler for Stalin.

The post-war world was volatile. In May 1946 Albanian artillery shelled British warships passing through the Corfu Channel, and when five months later a flotilla of destroyers passed through once more the destroyers *Saumarez* and *Volage* were badly damaged by mines. There was heavy loss of life, but in spite of a judgement in Britain's favour by the International Court of Justice no compensation for the 43 men killed was ever paid by the Albanians.

The Fleet Air Arm lost its proud title in 1946, taking on the nondescript name 'Naval Aviation' until the decision was rescinded seven years later. It was now the main striking force of the Fleet and led the way in several remarkable innovations. By the early 1950s the British had logged the first jet landing on a carrier, had tried out a flexible landing deck and had pioneered three major improvements: the steam catapult, the mirror landing sight and the angled flight deck. Looking back, the most remarkable point about these experiments is that they were carried out on a tiny budget.

There was innovation in other areas as well. In 1947 a motor gunboat went to sea with a Gatric gas turbine, and her trials were sufficiently successful for the Royal Navy to go ahead with long-term plans to change from steam propulsion to gas turbines. Many years later the historian of British marine gas turbines explained how it was that the United States Navy, which funded a large number of ideas, was still beaten by the Royal Navy. It was, he said, simply that the Royal Navy could only afford to back one candidate, and that happened to be the winner.

The Royal Navy also earned a fine reputation for its small escorts. As far back as 1944 plans had been drawn up for a series of standard mass-produced frigates, in which armament and equipment could be varied according to the role: anti-submarine, anti-aircraft or aircraft-direction. By 1950 this concept had evolved to the point when orders could be placed, and the outcome was the Type 12 frigate, still reckoned by many to be the finest escort produced by any Western navy since 1945. They were developed from the original *Whitby* Class through the *Rothesay* Class and culminated in the outstanding *Leander* design, which is still under development by India and the Netherlands. In all 69 frigates were built on the Type 12 hull and it formed the basis of a large class of Canadian destroyer escorts as well.

In other respects, however, the Royal Navy did not do well. The perennial shortage of funds meant that important items like guided missiles and new radars took far too long to come into service; time is money, and the protracted time to get weapons into service meant that it was all too often obsolete by the time it became operational. Short production-runs put up the cost, making British equipment harder to sell abroad, and the result was a growing tendency for the Treasury to cancel programmes which were overruning on cost.

The age of the battleship was over, but it was fitting that the last British 'battlewagon' should be the best of the breed. HMS *Vanguard* had, paradoxically, been

Above: Coxswain on duty at the after hydroplanes of the submarine *Cachalot* in 1977.

Below: The AA frigate *Mounts Bay* and her sisters served for many years in the post-war Fleet.

Left: A Sea King helicopter hovering over the *Resolution*, one of four Polaris SSBNs.

Right: The missile armed destroyer HMS *Birmingham*, second of the *Sheffield* class.

Below: The FRS.1 Sea Harrier is an improved version of the vertical takeoff support aircraft used by the RAF and US Marine Corps.

planned as early as 1938 to provide a fast battleship to counter the Japanese in the Far East. In 1940 it was realised that no new triple 16-inch gun turrets could be manufactured before 1944 at the earliest, and the Director of Naval Ordnance had suggested that four of the superb 15-inch gun turrets, stripped from the light battle-cruisers *Courageous* and *Glorious* when they were converted to carriers in the 1920s, could be used instead. Wartime shortages delayed the ship, and although strenuous efforts were made to get her ready for the Pacific she did not emerge until 1946. For a while the old *Nelson* and three of the *King George V* Class remained in commission, but by 1950 the *Vanguard* was the last battleship to remain operational. To many who had known the old Royal Navy – always the 'Andrew' to old matelots – it was a sad break with the past when in 1948 such veterans as the *Queen Elizabeth, Valiant, Nelson* and *Rodney* went to the breakers. But, quite apart from their age and war-weariness, the battleships absorbed too much manpower to justify their retention.

In July 1950 the appeal by the United States for an international effort to defend South Korea against Communist aggression was met by the formation of a Commonwealth Task Force. The Royal Navy was able to send the following ships:

Light fleet carriers: *Glory, Ocean, Theseus, Triumph, Unicorn* and *Warrior*
Cruisers: *Belfast, Birmingham, Ceylon, Jamaica, Kenya, Newcastle* and *Newfoundland*
Destroyers: *Charity, Cockade, Comus, Concord, Consort, Constance, Cossack* and *Defender*
Frigates: *Alacrity, Alert, Amethyst, Black Swan, Cardigan Bay, Crane, Hart, Modeste, Morecambe Bay, Mounts Bay, Opossum, St Bride's Bay, Sparrow* and *Whitesand Bay*
Submarines: *Tactician* and *Telemachus*
Depot ships: *Tyne* and *Ladybird*

To support a large number of warships so far from a main base (although Japanese facilities were available) it was necessary to deploy four stores ships, 12 fleet oilers and the hospital ship *Maine* (reviving a traditional name for hospital ships, commemorating a ship chartered by American ladies during the Boer War). Also serving with the British ships were Australian, New Zealand and Canadian warships:

Light fleet carriers: HMAS *Sydney*
Destroyers: HMASs *Anzac, Bataan, Tobruk* and *Warramunga*
HMCSs *Athabaskan, Cayuga, Crusader, Haida, Huron, Iroquois, Nootka* and *Sioux*
Frigates: HMASs *Condamine, Culgoa, Murchison* and *Shoalhaven*
HMNZSs *Hawea, Kaniere, Pukaki, Rotoiti, Taupo* and *Tutira*

It was a long, arduous and ultimately frustrating war, but it was ample proof of the value of carriers in supporting land operations. Week in, week out, the light fleet carriers launched their Sea Furies, Fireflies and Seafires to operate over land, while the cruisers, destroyers and frigates bombarded shore positions in response to calls for gunfire support. Nor was it a safe task, for several ships were damaged by shore batteries. In August 1952 a formation of four Sea Furies from HMS *Ocean* was 'jumped' by MiG-15 jet fighters. When it is considered that the MiG-15 was at least 190 knots faster than the propeller-driven Sea Fury the reaction of the naval pilots was remarkable: one MiG was shot down and two more were damaged.

In 1956 the Royal Navy was called upon to mount an even more massive operation, the operations to occupy the Suez Canal Zone. It would be tedious to recall the tortuous political background to the Suez Crisis, or the rights and wrongs of the

Below: The battleship *Anson* leaving the Gareloch on her way to be scrapped in 1958.

matter, but suffice it to say that the brunt fell on the Navy. A carrier task force existed, but in addition troops and heavy equipment had to be brought out from England, using Malta and Cyprus as staging posts. As an added burden the Royal Marine Commandos were to be sent into action by helicopter for the first time; the technique of 'vertical envelopment' had been practiced by the US Marine Corps but the British had no ships or helicopters dedicated to this role.

The Suez Canal was nationalized by President Nasser at the end of July 1956, and over the next two months reinforcements were sent out to the Mediterranean Fleet. The light fleet carriers *Ocean* and *Theseus* were hurriedly converted to assault ships, with temporary accommodation for Marine Commandos and the normal air group replaced by helicopters.

By 29th October it was reported that a large Anglo-French naval force was operating in the Eastern Mediterranean. Next day the British and French governments published their ultimatum to the Egyptians and Israelis, ordering them to withdraw 10 miles from either side of the Canal. Subsequently it was to be charged that the British and French were in collusion with the Israeli forces, but as far as the

Royal Navy was concerned it had a job to do, and on the night of 31st October, hostilities began in earnest. The cruiser HMS *Newfoundland* detected a ship on radar off the southern end of the Canal, and when she challenged the newcomer she saw gunflashes. Two shells struck the cruiser, killing one sailor and wounding five but no serious damage resulted; she was closed up at action stations and within seconds the 6-inch guns replied. Six minutes of firing ended with the sinking of the Egyptian frigate *Domiat*. The *Newfoundland* picked up 69 survivors from the plucky little frigate, which had tried to match the cruiser's nine 6-inch guns with two 4-inch.

Shortly after this action the frigate *Crane* was attacked by four Israeli aircraft and shot one of them down before the action was broken off. Next morning the French and British carriers started a series of air raids on targets ashore. In two days the Fleet Air Arm flew 355 sorties and an estimated total of 71 Egyptian aircraft was destroyed. Losses were comparatively light: a Wyvern torpedo-bomber and two Sea Hawk interceptors lost in the first four days. On 5th November the paratroop landing was made but a day later the Navy faced the sterner test of a

helicopter landing from the *Ocean* and *Theseus*, which were carrying Royal Marine Commandos.

As the world's first helicopter assault it went remarkably smoothly. The helicopters returned to the carriers to reload, taking only a minute to get the marines on board, and after every second trip they refuelled, a job which took four minutes. As soon as all the marines were ashore the helicopters started to evacuate casualties, and it is claimed that one wounded man was back in the sickbay of HMS *Theseus* only 20 minutes after he had left.

The British and French withdrew at American insistence, and so the whole Suez operation was a fruitless endeavour. The RN, however, could look with some satisfaction on the way in which it had met the totally unexpected call to mobilise. In all 105 warships and Royal Fleet Auxiliaries took part and 50 requisitioned merchant ships were involved, 14 Fleet Air Arm squadrons and 20,000 men. The Navy had taken the Egyptians by surprise and had suffered no losses, despite the hazards of an opposed landing. What had been lacking was political will, not military competence.

The British armed forces were in bitter mood after Suez for they felt with some

justification that they had been committed to a dangerous enterprise and had then been let down just when victory seemed certain. But they were heading for a much more serious humiliation. In 1957, the year in which the first British hydrogen bomb was tested, the Conservative government's Defence Minister Duncan Sandys announced a large cutback in all three Services. In a tragically short-sighted moment Sandys put his name to a document which stated, among other things, that the future role of naval forces was 'uncertain' and that there could be no future for the manned military aircraft. The 'Sandys White Paper' took it for granted that nuclear war was inevitable, and made no mention of the growing Russian fleet of surface warships and submarines. All research on guns was stopped, a decision which was still being regretted 25 years later, when the Navy found that it had no designs for close range anti-aircraft guns.

The Sandys Axe had some benefits, however. The Reserve Fleet of some 550 ships was abolished, and as much of the money spent was going towards refits of worn-out Second World War ships and the maintenance of five battleships, it freed funds for new construction. A new urgency was given to developing missiles for the Fleet, and the building of nuclear-powered submarines was to be accelerated. There was also a 'bulge' in the numbers of the officer corps, particularly among the admirals and commanders, partly the result of the Korean War mobilisation, and some drastic pruning was needed to provide promotion prospects for the remainder. Another long-term benefit was the greater emphasis on 'afloat support', the use of tankers and supply ships rather than shore bases, which might be knocked out by nuclear attack.

It must be remembered that Western strategic planners (and their political masters) thought that the Cold War was almost certain to change to a 'Hot War' in the late 1950s. In 1957 there were thought to be 100 ocean-going diesel-electric boats, six new cruisers, 40-50 destroyers and escorts, and 700 naval aircraft in the Soviet Navy. There was no news yet of the rise of Admiral Sergei Gorshkov, but the portents of the remarkable growth of Soviet sea power were already discernible.

The British Government had insisted on maintaining its own nuclear deterrent, in order to reduce the risk of the United States abandoning its European allies. Threats from the Soviet Union at the time of Suez lent some substance to these fears, and a force of nuclear bombers was built up by the Air Force. By 1964 the question of modernising the weaponry of this 'V-

Right: The frigate *Arethusa* refuelling from HMS *Albion* in the Bay of Bengal, December 1971.

Bomber' force was under discussion, but when the US Air Force cancelled its projected Skybolt air-launched ballistic missile the British Government had to make a painful decision, either to drop the deterrent or find another weapon system. The United States came to the rescue by offering the A-3 Polaris missile system at a reasonable price, and so the Royal Navy once more resumed its place as the principal guardian of the nation's security. Four nuclear submarines were built in British shipyards, each armed with 16 Polaris missiles capable of hitting targets deep inside Russia. Like their American counterparts they adopted double crewing, with Port and Starboard crews changing over at the end of each patrol.

By 1980 Polaris needed replacement, and once again the Royal Navy turned to the United States. It is planned to buy Trident II missiles for installation in four new nuclear submarines, but unlike the Polaris purchase the decision has been fiercely attacked, not just by opponents of nuclear weapons but by some defence experts as well. The biggest drawback is Trident's cost, which this time must be borne by the Royal Navy alone, whereas Polaris costs were shared in a tri-service 'strategic vote'. Many defence planners fear that the enormous outlay on Trident will only result in the Navy losing yet more of its conventional forces. What also angered many was the furtive way in which the updating of the Polaris warheads, a project code-named 'Chevaline', was funded. Nothing was known about Chevaline until the money had been spent, the money had been 'lost' among five years of Naval Estimates. The four Trident submarines, named *Vanguard, Venerable, Victorious* and *Vengeance*, will come into service in the early 1990s, replacing the four *Resolution* class.

Although the use of helicopters from ships at sea had been tried in 1943-44 they were still widely regarded as too frail and unreliable to be employed extensively. The Royal Navy, however, thought differently and 1957 saw the first deployment of a light helicopter on board an anti-submarine frigate, HMS *Grenville*. Out of these trials emerged the concept of using a light helicopter to drop depth-charges or homing torpedoes on a submarine, and by the early 1960s all Royal Navy frigates and destroyers were being equipped with this system, and other navies were copying it. Today no major warship is built without helicopter facilities.

In many ways the Navy's tasks on the high seas had not changed since the days of Queen Victoria, and there was a constant recurrence of minor acts of lawlessness and mishaps requiring the presence of a warship. As early as 1949 the frigate *Amethyst* had been held prisoner by Chinese Communist troops on the Yangtze, and the Malayan Emergency had provided the Navy with an opportunity to support British and Commonwealth land forces in putting down a Communist uprising. In 1963 relations between Great Britain and Indonesia began to deteriorate. The Indonesian Government was actively supporting subversion in Borneo, and the Malaysian Government had called on Great Britain as the guarantor of external security to help her defend her territory. As in Malaya itself, the British forces proved adept at running a 'Hearts and Minds' campaign to win the support of local Iban tribesmen, with the result that the Indonesians' movements were constantly reported to the British.

One of the most remarkable aspects of the campaign was the work of Naval Party Kilo, a scratch force of river craft known as kotaks, which were armed with a light machine gun to patrol the rivers and swamps of Sarawak. Force Kilo was based

Above: The carrier *Ark Royal*, cruiser *Blake*, DLG *Hampshire*, frigates *Lowestoft, Achilles, Falmouth, Diomede* and *Leander*, with two RFAs and Brazilian warships, during a May 1975 exercise.

Left: The commando carrier *Albion* operating off Northern Norway in September 1972.

at Kuching, from where it patrolled for up to 10 days at a time, moving Royal Marines or Gurkhas to places where hostile activity was reported or simply watching the movements of local craft and stopping infiltration. In time the kotaks were replaced by assault landing craft or stores tenders, and under a variety of unofficial names they became the strangest craft ever to fly the White Ensign.

Quasi-wars always provide the most anomalous situations. The British and Australian Governments had no intention of starting a war with the Republic of Indonesia, but equally could not watch a stable Commonwealth state overthrown by Indonesian subversion. By March 1965 it looked as if war could not be avoided, when three RN coastal minesweepers sank one landing craft and damaged

another, off Southern Malaya. During that year the various Australian and British warships steamed a million miles and killed or captured over 1400 Indonesian raiders, at a cost of two men killed and 11 injured. Not until the summer of 1966 did the Indonesians finally admit that they could not win 'Confrontation', and by September that year the last British warship had been withdrawn from Borneo.

Only nine years after the Sandys Axe the Labour Government was about to administer an equally savage blow to the Royal Navy. The Defence Minister, Mr Denis Healey, presented a White Paper to Parliament in which he proposed the abolition of aircraft carriers and the Fleet Air Arm. Instead guided missiles would provide fleet air defence, while helicopters would continue to provide anti-submarine screening and a limited strike capability. Overall air defence would be provided by the Royal Air Force, flying from bases in Great Britain or from as yet unbuilt island bases in the Indian Ocean. The carrier, it was asserted, could easily be knocked out by long-range missiles, and in any case the alternatives already

mentioned were more cost-effective.

As always the arguments proved to be founded on more false premises than facts; to prove that F-111 bombers could fly from Western Australia to India one RAF policy document was later discovered to have 'moved Australia' 400 miles closer to India to get over an inconvenient shortfall in the range. The totally inaccurate idea that intercontinental missiles can be targeted on aircraft carriers at sea was planted in Mr Healey's mind (if true, they could also destroy Air Force bases, but nobody mentioned that). But above all the costings were grossly inaccurate. It was subsequently revealed that the cost of developing the island bases would have been double the cost of the projected carrier *CVA.01*. During the debate Mr Healey put figures before Parliament regarding the cost of a new carrier which later turned out to include the cost of a *second* carrier and four new missile-armed destroyers which were to escort them.

In the long run the RAF was forced to give up not only its excellent TSR.2 supersonic bomber but also its replacement, the

American F-111 bomber. The attempt to provide the Navy with shore-based air support proved too much for the RAF; even with the Phantom interceptors transferred from the Fleet Air Arm the added commitment was too much for an already over-stretched service.

Notwithstanding all the evidence, particularly from American experience, that there was no real alternative to the flexibility of seaborne air power, the plans to sink the Fleet Air Arm went on apace. The carrier *Victorious* suffered a small fire during a refit, and was certified as 'beyond repair' with suspicious haste. Then the newly modernised carrier *Eagle* was pronounced to be not worth converting to Phantom aircraft; she was laid up while her less modern, unmodified sister *Ark Royal* was to run until 1972 as the only strike carrier. The smaller carriers *Albion* and *Bulwark* had already been converted to commando ships (helicopter carriers) and the *Hermes* was to join them. To make absolutely certain that a future government could not reverse the decision the *Eagle* was stripped of catapults and arrester gear (a high-level order had

The Royal Navy's first nuclear-powered submarine, HMS *Dreadnought*, leaving Faslane. Her reactor was supplied by the US Navy but later SSNs use British reactors.

already been given to destroy all drawings of *CVA.01*, presumably for similar reasons).

The Fleet Air Arm showed a remarkable resilience, and when in due course it proved impossible to dispense with the old *Ark*'s services the Government was forced to admit that she would have to serve until 1978, by which time a new type of carrier (that same type of ship officially presumed useless) might be ready. In fact the genesis of this new type of carrier actually predated the 1966 Defence Review.

To provide the new carrier *CVA.01* with a bigger complement of strike aircraft and interceptors it had been proposed to build a helicopter carrier to house the anti-submarine helicopters. After 1966 thoughts turned to the possibility of building a 'command cruiser' armed with missiles for the air defence of a task group and equipped with elaborate communications and radar to control operations over a wide area. Clearly both functions would be economically combined in one ship, and when British Aerospace announced the design of a naval version of the already famous Harrier Vertical/Short Takeoff and Landing (V/STOL) aircraft it even seemed possible that fixed-wing aviation might be saved. However, just as had happened in 1936-37, the politicians shrank from admitting that they had made a mistake, and to avoid the Defence Minister's wrath the ludicrous euphemism 'Through Deck Cruiser' had to be coined for the new ship. It was also impossible to get the Government to make up its mind about the new Sea Harrier, and so although the ship had been designed with the Sea Harrier in mind it continued to be referred to as a helicopter-operating ship and the order for the Sea Harrier was delayed until the last possible moment.

The ship, named the *Invincible*, was duly launched by HM the Queen in May 1977, the year of her Silver Jubilee, and she went to sea for the first time three years later. She was not only a new and unorthodox type of light carrier but also the world's largest warship driven solely by gas turbines, with four Olympus turbines driving two propeller shafts. Two sisters were ordered in 1976 and 1978, *Illustrious* and *Ark Royal* (formerly *Indomitable*), and all three were given a new invention, the Ski Jump. This invention by a Royal Navy engineer officer, allows a Sea Harrier to make a 'rolling takeoff' (as against a vertical takeoff) with up to 1500lbs more fuel or ordnance on board.

With other new classes of warship coming forward and a new role to provide anti-submarine patrols in the Greenland-Iceland-UK Gap it seemed that at last the Royal Navy could look forward to an assured future, but in June 1981 the Conservative Defence Minister, Mr John Nott, announced sweeping reductions in the Royal Navy's surface fleet. In the heroic mould of Duncan Sandys and Denis Healey he announced that defence against Soviet nuclear submarines could be safely left to nuclear submarines and RAF Nimrod maritime patrol aircraft. The new carrier *Invincible* would be offered for sale to Australia and a role for the remaining two 'might be found' outside the North Atlantic. All the older frigates and destroyers would be scrapped or sold immediately and the amphibious warfare ships would no longer be needed.

For once public opinion seems to have been stirred, and considerable alarm was expressed, not just in Britain but in NATO and the United States, for the Royal Navy provided 70 per cent of the forces in the Eastern Atlantic. However, Mr Nott stuck to his guns, and insisted that the cuts should go ahead, and the Royal Australian Navy prepared to receive its new flagship HMAS *Australia*. The British Government was still beset by economic problems thanks to the world-wide recession, and its answer to all criticism was that economies had to be made. The real problem was that a British Army presence in Germany had become a sacred cow; critics of the Navy cuts argue that if all the dependants of the British army of the Rhine were housed and looked after at home scarce foreign currency would be saved. After all, troops' dependants are not sent to Northern Ireland and the Navy and the Air Force have to go abroad without requiring schools, married quarters and shops to be provided. Certainly the commitment to support NATO with ground troops cannot be cancelled, for valid political reasons, but a rapid deployment force would be a more effective use of the manpower, and it would also enable the defence budget to be balanced more easily.

The story of the Royal Navy might have ended on that depressing note but for a remarkable series of events which started in the spring of 1982.

The Falkland Islands lie some 400 miles off the coast of Chile and Argentina. They had already played an important role in Britain's naval past, in November 1914 when British capital ships arrived in time to fend off a German attack, and in

December 1939 when the heavy cruiser *Exeter* carried out urgent repairs to damage sustained during the Battle of the River Plate. The islands were discovered by an Englishman as long ago as 1592, but in 1706 the first Breton sailors arrived to settle there and called them *Les Malouines*, after their home port St Malo.

This settlement was abandoned after eight years but in 1764 the British and French each laid claim to part of the islands. Both claims were denied by Spain in 1767, on the grounds that the islands were an offshoot of their mainland possessions. The French acquiesced and sold their settlement back to Spain but it took military action by the Spanish to suppress the British settlement at Port Egmont. As a result of diplomatic protests the action was repudiated by Spain, and in 1810 the Spanish garrison was withdrawn to help deal with the war of independence which had started on the mainland.

There things might have rested had not the newly independent nation of Argentina decided in 1820 to reoccupy the islands, known in Spanish as *Las*

Malvinas. A small party from the schooner *Heroina* landed and hoisted the Argentine flag. Only in 1831 did the British decide to reassert their claim and the Argentine settlers were expelled by landing parties from two warships. Settlers were brought from Britain, and from then until 1914 they farmed sheep with little or no interference from the outside world. The capital Port Stanley was, however, strategically important as a coaling station and as a link in the world-wide submarine cable system. And this is why Admiral von Spee wished to attack the Falklands in 1914.

The claim had never been abandoned by Argentina, and since 1945 it had become a constant theme in Anglo-Argentine relations, to the point where neither side cared what the islands were worth. There were several unofficial attempts by groups of patriots to hoist the Argentine flag on the islands, but each time they were removed peacefully and expelled. However, in 1977, with Argentina under the control of a military junta, there was an attempt at a military take-

over; this was only frustrated by a show of strength by the British Government, which sent warships and submarines to the South Atlantic for well-timed 'exercises'. No such foresight distinguished British conduct in 1982, for discussions with the Foreign Office had left the Argentines in no doubt that the British wished to be rid of the Falklands, and sooner rather than later. Among Mr Nott's cuts was the scrapping of the Antarctic patrol ship *Endurance*, which, it was announced, would not be replaced. Nor can there be any doubt that the cuts in the Royal Navy would have seriously impaired the Royal Navy's ability to do anything about the Falklands, even if it wanted to. Among the ships up for sale was the amphibious assault ship *Intrepid*, and she had been offered to Argentina!

Rumours of Argentine moves against the Falklands grew stronger at the end of

Below: The DDG *Sheffield* leaving Barrow in Furness on trials in 1974. Eight years later she was sunk by an Argentine missile in the Falklands.

D23

Above: The DLG *Bristol*, survivor of four large escorts intended to work with the cancelled carriers *CVA.01* and *CVA.02*.

March 1982 and on 2nd April the British press reported that an invasion was actually in progress, although the Government and the Foreign Office appeared to know nothing about it. By next day TV film confirmed the presence of armoured vehicles in Port Stanley, and the Prime Minister Mrs Thatcher announced that a Task Force would be formed to recover the islands.

The result is now history, for despite tribulations it ended in a stunning victory, but in military terms it was a nightmare. To get together a task force and send it 8000 miles down into the South Atlantic winter would strain men and ships to their limit, even if no fighting occurred. The nearest base would be at Ascension Island, 4000 miles away, making it impossible to carry out anything but minor repairs locally. Nor should it be forgotten that the Falklands were within reach of air bases in Southern Argentina, and that Argentina's armed forces possessed modern weapons.

Against all the odds the main part of the Task Force was ready to sail within 72 hours, led by the flagship *Hermes* and appropriately the *Invincible*, carrying Sea King helicopters and Sea Harrier aircraft. Other ships followed as soon as they could, some like the *Intrepid* having been destored before being taken out of service. The commander of the Task Force was Rear-Admiral John 'Sandy' Woodward, formerly the Flag Officer, First

Flotilla, and the operation was code-named 'Corporate'.

A feature of the operation was the rapid conversion of a wide variety of merchant ships. Apart from a number of oil tankers needed to freight fuel to Ascension there were ferries and container ships. For the first time two roll-on/roll-off ships, the *Atlantic Causeway* and *Atlantic Conveyor* were converted to operate aircraft, the former having a hangar accommodating four Sea King helicopters and the latter having a flight deck protected by windbreaks made out of containers. In addition their vast vehicle decks were packed with military equipment, including a portable airfield and refuelling equipment to be set up ashore.

On 27th April a small advance force comprising HMS *Antrim*, *Brilliant* and *Plymouth* and the supply ship *Tidespring* put Royal Marines ashore at Grytviken in South Georgia. This inhospitable little island is a long way from the Falklands but it provided a useful forward base for units of the Task Force, and its capture was the first good news which the British had had since 2nd April. A day later the formation of a Total Exclusion Zone around the Falklands was announced. Like a blockade, it gave the British the right to treat any ship or aircraft in the area as hostile, including aircraft on Falklands airfields.

The first military action against the Falklands was an ineffective raid by an RAF Vulcan bomber on 1st May – it was a meagre result for a spectacular piece of flying, a round trip of 7000 miles. Later the Vulcans on Ascension were to mount a more useful series of operations known as 'Black Buck', using American Shrike anti-radar missiles to try to knock out Argentine radars, and leaving the job of bombing ground targets to the Harriers and Sea Harriers. On 4th May a second Vulcan raid was followed by an attack from Sea Harriers, an indication that the Task Force carriers were now within striking range.

Up until 2nd May there was every chance that both sides might find, with the help of the United States, a peaceful solution to the dispute, but that day the nuclear submarine HMS *Conqueror* was given permission to torpedo the old *General Belgrano*, which was apparently part of a three-pronged surface attack on the Task Force. The 44-year-old veteran of Pearl Harbor sank quickly with the loss of some 350 men, rousing great indignation in Argentina. Two days later the Argentines evened the score, when a French-built Super Etendard naval strike aircraft from the mainland hit the destroyer HMS *Sheffield* with an AM.39 Exocet guided missile. Horrified onlookers from the flagship *Hermes* saw a huge column of smoke on the horizon as the stricken ship's fuel tanks caught fire, and the ship continued to burn as the firefighters lost control. Eventually she was abandoned and allowed to burn herself out. There was talk of towing her to South Georgia but on 10th May she gave up the struggle as the weather worsened and she was finally scuttled, along with an Argentine trawler captured in the Total Exclusion Zone.

Despite the loss of the *Sheffield* the Task Force continued to tighten its grip on the Falklands, and on the night of 13th/14th May a special force landed on Pebble Island and destroyed an estimated 11 aircraft, munitions and fuel. After a long reconnaissance the naval and land commanders chose their spot for the main landing, and at about 8.30 on the morning of 21st May the first ships arrived off Port San Carlos on the north-western side of East Falkland. Total surprise had been achieved and the troops were safely ashore before the Argentine Air Force could react. However, with a number of Pucará ground-attack aircraft deployed on local airstrips and the mainland bases only half an hour's flying time away, retaliation was swift. As many as 72 aircraft were reported over San Carlos Water on the first day and the Argentine pilots showed incredible bravery as they dived to as little as 50 ft. During the next hectic days 'Bomb Alley' was the scene of an air-sea battle of a ferocity not seen since 1945. The British Sea Harriers were too few in number to stop all the Mirages and Skyhawks from getting through, and the destroyer *Coventry*, the frigates *Antelope* and *Ardent* and the merchant ship *Atlantic Conveyor* were sunk. The main problem was that the Navy's missiles forced the Argentine pilots to fly very low, but at low altitude the ship's radars could not pick up the targets quickly and they lacked close-range guns or missiles which could have saved them. Only two

ships, the frigates *Brilliant* and *Broadsword* had the new Seawolf missile, and they could only make a limited contribution to air defence. Finally, however, the sting went out of the air attacks as the Argentine Air Force lost an estimated 34 Mirages and Skyhawks. A large number of British ships were hit by bombs but fortunately the aircraft were flying so low that the majority of bombs failed to arm themselves and so did not explode.

The land battle went successfully after paratroops and marines broke out of the bridgehead and captured the airfield at Goose Green. Then began a remarkable march across wild country to Port Stanley. The only bad setback was the failure of an attempt to run two landing ships carrying troops into Bluff Cove, a small harbour on the south-eastern coast. The two landing ships were without air cover and rashly remained in the cove after daybreak; Argentine lookouts on high ground spotted them and within a short while aircraft had set them both on fire, killing 51 men and wounding many. But by 9th June the fate of the Argentine garrison was sealed, with all the high ground in British hands. The Navy's luck continued to hold, and even an Exocet hit on the destroyer *Glamorgan* two days before the end did not sink the ship. She was hit right at the end of the missile's run, and although 13 men were killed and 14 wounded in the galley underneath the deck, and the helicopter hangar was wrecked the ship was not knocked out. On the night of 13th/14th June the Argentine commander General Menendez asked for an armistice and the following day he and 11,000 troops surrendered.

It had been a remarkable campaign in which the small but sophisticated Task

Force had taken a number of chances. The chief lack on the British side was of airborne early warning aircraft which had formerly been operated by carriers like the *Ark Royal*. The new carriers had no provision for this sort of aircraft, and the Ski Jump ramp in any case would have prevented the old Gannet AEW aircraft from flying off their decks. There was also a lack of close-range anti-aircraft weaponry, for over the years it had been assumed that the Royal Navy would always be operating in the Atlantic, far from shore-based strike aircraft. Fortunately the vital amphibious warfare element was still intact, but had the Argentines waited another six months the assault ships would have been sold or scrapped, the carriers *Hermes* and *Invincible* would also have been sold.

It is impossible to say what the future of the Royal Navy will be, but in the light of events in the Falklands future governments will have difficulty in continuing with a policy of abandoning all the functions of the surface fleet. From time to time Britain's rulers have foolishly tried to manage without a strong Navy and each time their folly has been exposed. Things have not changed much since the 17th century, when the men who framed the Naval Discipline Act started with the assumption that 'it is on the Navy that the health and safety of the realm do chiefly depend.' Every time the Navy has been weak Britain has suffered disaster, and every time the Navy has been efficient the nation's fortunes have prospered. Surely so much history cannot be ignored.

Below: The gas turbine-driven *Brave Borderer*, one of the last fast patrol boats to serve in the Royal Navy.

Index

Acknowledgements

The Admiralty 132, 158, 163, 166
British Aerospace Aircraft Group 174
Charles E. Brown 164
Conway Picture Library 162
Lt. Gustave J. Freret USN (Ret.) 132, 137
Wallace Heaton 174
Robert Hunt 114, 121 (Bottom), 159 (Center)
Imperial War Museum 111 (Top), 119 (Top),
  120 (Bottom, Top left), 122 (Top left), 124,
  125, 128, 132, 136, 143 (Top), 147, 154, 161
  (Bottom), 168
Humphrey Joel 130 (Bottom)
Mayo Ltd 131 (Top)
Ministry of Defence 60, 174, 175, 180
National Archives 136
National Maritime Museum 12, 13 (Bottom),
  14 (Top), 15, 18, 20, 22, 23, 24, 25 (Bottom),
  26, 27, 28, 30, 31, 32, 34, 35, 36, 37, 38, 39, 40,
  41, 42, 44, 45, 46, 47, 48, 49, 50, 51, 52, 53, 55,
  56, 57, 58, 61, 62 (Center), 63, 64, 66, 67, 68,
  70, 71, 72, 75, 76, 77 (Bottom), 78, 79, 80, 81,
  82, 83, 84, 85 (Top, Bottom), 86, 87, 88, 89,
  90, 92, 93, 94, 95, 96, 98, 100, 103, 104, 105,
  108, 109, 113 (Top right), 117, 121 (Top),
  127, 131 (Bottom), 138 (Bottom), 146 (Top),
  152 (Top), 153 (Top), 156 (Top), 166 (Top
  left)
Naval Institute 132
Newark Public Library Picture Collection 10
A. Preston 142, 144, 155
Royal Naval Air Services 130 (Top)
Science Museum 16
CPO Eric Thompson FOSM 173
US Navy 141
US Naval Historical Center (D. McPherson)
  139 (Top)